Dinah Zike's
Reading and Study Skills

FOLDABLES™

Dinah Zike's
Reading and Study Skills
FOLDABLES™

OUR WORLD TODAY
People, Places, and Issues

- 3-D, interactive graphic organizers
- Hands-on manipulatives
- Reading and study-skill strategies, review, and assessment
- Makes Social Studies accessible to all students

Mc Graw Hill **Glencoe McGraw-Hill**

New York, New York   Columbus, Ohio   Chicago, Illinois   Peoria, Illinois   Woodland Hills, California

Glencoe/McGraw-Hill

A Division of The **McGraw·Hill** *Companies*

Send all inquiries to:
Glencoe/McGraw-Hill
8787 Orion Place
Columbus, OH 43240-4027

ISBN 0-07-829365-0

Printed in the United States of America

1 2 3 4 5 6 7 8 9 10   079   08 07 06 05 04 03 02

Table of Contents

Letter From Dinah Zike 1

Introduction to Foldables

Why Use Foldables in Social Studies? 2
Foldables and the NCSS Thematic Strands 2
Foldable Basics 3
Using Visuals and Graphics With Foldables 5

Folding Instructions

Basic Foldables Shapes 13
Half Book 14
Folded Book 15
Three-Quarter Book 16
Bound Book 17
Two-Tab Book 18
Pocket Book 19
Matchbook 20
Shutter Fold 21
Trifold Book 22
Three-Tab Book 23
Pyramid Fold 24
Layered-Look Book 25
Four-Tab Book 26
Standing Cube 27
Envelope Fold 28
Four-Door Book 29
Top-Tab Book 30

Accordion Book 32
Pop-Up Book 33
Five-Tab Book 34
Folded Table or Chart 35
Folding a Circle Into Tenths 36
Circle Graph 37
Concept-Map Book 38
Vocabulary Book 39
Four-Door Diorama 40
Picture Frame Book 41
Display Case 42
Billboard Project 43
Project Board With Tabs 44
Sentence Strips 45
Sentence-Strip Holder 46
Forward-Backward Book 47
Three-Pocket Book 48

Chapter-Specific Foldables 49

Chapter 1 Our Social World 50

Chapter 2 Earth Patterns 52

Chapter 3 North Africa and Southwest Asia—
Early Cultures 54

Chapter 4 North Africa and Southwest Asia Today 56

Chapter 5 South Asia 58

Chapter 6 China and Its Neighbors 60

Chapter 7 Japan and the Koreas 62

Chapter 8 Southeast Asia 64

Chapter 9 Europe—Early History 66

Chapter 10 Europe—Modern History 68

Chapter 11 Western Europe Today 70

Chapter 12 Eastern Europe Today 72

Chapter 13 Russia and Its Neighbors 74

Chapter 14 Russia—Past and Present 76

Chapter 15 East and Central Africa 78

Chapter 16 West Africa 80

Chapter 17 South Africa and Its Neighbors 82

Chapter 18 Canada 84

Chapter 19 The United States 86

Chapter 20 Mexico 88

Chapter 21 Central America and the West Indies 90

Chapter 22 Brazil and Its Neighbors 92

Chapter 23 The Andean Countries 94

Chapter 24 Australia and New Zealand 96

Chapter 25 Oceania and Antarctica 98

Dear Teacher,

What is a Foldable?

A Foldable is a 3-D, student-made, interactive graphic organizer based upon a skill. Making a Foldable gives students a fast, kinesthetic activity that helps them organize and retain information. Every chapter in the student edition of the textbook begins with a Foldable that is used as a Study Organizer. Each chapter's Foldable is designed to be used as a study guide for the main ideas and key points presented in sections of the chapter. Foldables can also be used for a more in-depth investigation of a concept, idea, opinion, event, or a person or place studied in a chapter. The purpose of this ancillary is to show you how to create various types of Foldables and provide chapter-specific Foldables examples. With this information, you can individualize Foldables to meet your curriculum needs.

This book is divided into two sections. The first section presents step-by-step instructions, illustrations, and photographs of 34 Foldables, many of which were not used in the student edition. I've included over 100 photographs to help you visualize ways in which they might enhance instruction. The second section presents two extra ideas on how to use Foldables for each chapter in the textbook. You can use the instruction section to design your own Foldables or alter the Foldables presented in each chapter as well. I highly suggest making this book available as a source for students who wish to learn new and creative ways in which to make study guides, present projects, or do extra credit work.

Who Am I?

You may have seen Foldables featured in this book used in supplemental programs or staff-development workshops. Today my Foldables are used internationally. I present workshops and keynotes to over fifty thousand teachers and parents a year, sharing Foldables that I began inventing, designing, and adapting over thirty five years ago. Students of all ages are using them for daily work, note-taking activities, student-directed projects, forms of alternative assessment, journals, graphs, tables, and more.

Have fun using and adapting Foldables,

Dinah Zike

Why use Foldables in Social Studies?

When teachers ask me why they should take time to use the Foldables featured in this book, I explain that they:

. . . organize, display, and arrange information, making it easier for students to grasp social studies concepts, theories, facts, opinions, questions, research, and ideas.

. . . are student-made study guides that are compiled as students listen for main ideas, read for main ideas, or conduct research.

. . . provide a multitude of creative formats in which students can present projects, research, interviews, and inquiry-based reports.

. . . replace teacher-generated writing or photocopied sheets with student-generated print.

. . . incorporate the use of such skills as comparing and contrasting, recognizing cause and effect, and finding similarities and differences.

. . . continue to "immerse" students in previously learned vocabulary, concepts, information, generalizations, ideas, and theories, providing them with a strong foundation that they can build upon with new observations, concepts, and knowledge.

. . . can be used by students or teachers to easily communicate data through graphs, tables, charts, models, and diagrams, including Venn diagrams.

. . . allow students to make their own journals for recording observations, research information, primary and secondary source data, surveys, and so on.

. . . can be used as alternative assessment tools by teachers to evaluate student progress or by students to evaluate their own progress.

. . . integrate language arts, the sciences, and mathematics into the study of social studies.

. . . provide a sense of student ownership or investiture in the social studies curriculum.

Foldables and the NCSS Thematic Strands

In *Curriculum Standards for Social Studies: Expectations of Excellence,* the National Council for the Social Studies (NCSS) identified 10 themes that serve as organizing strands for the social studies curriculum at every school level. The themes include:

I.   Culture
II.   Time, Continuity, and Change
III.   People, Places, and Environments
IV.   Individual Development and Identity
V.   Individuals, Groups, and Institutions
VI.   Power, Authority, and Governance
VII.   Production, Distribution, and Consumption
VIII.   Science, Technology, and Society
IX.   Global Connections
X.   Civic Ideals and Practices

Students are expected to master specific skills that are organized around these themes, such as analyzing data, comparing and contrasting similarities and differences, explaining and describing concepts, and identifying cause-and-effect relationships.

Foldables help students practice and master these specific skills. Foldables require students to identify and describe main ideas, relationships, and processes. In most cases, students need to understand and comprehend information before they can illustrate it in a foldable. Foldables help students think, analyze, and communicate.

Foldable Basics

What to Write and Where

Teach students to write general information such as titles, vocabulary words, concepts, questions, main ideas, and dates on the front tabs of their Foldables. This way students can easily recognize main ideas and important concepts. Foldables help students focus on and remember key points without being distracted by other print.

Ask students to write specific information such as supporting ideas, student thoughts, answers to questions, research information, class notes, observations, and definitions under the tabs.

As you teach, demonstrate different ways in which Foldables can be used. Soon you will find that students make their own Foldables and use them independently for study guides and projects.

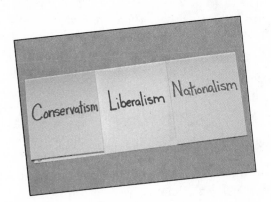

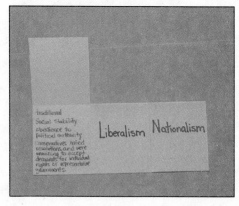

With or Without Tabs

Foldables with flaps or tabs create study guides that students can use to check what they know about the general information on the front of tabs. Use Foldables without tabs for assessment purposes or projects where information is presented for others to view quickly.

Venn diagram used as a study guide

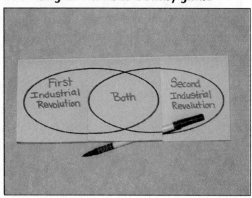

Venn diagram used for assessment

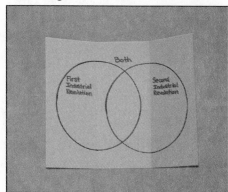

What to Do With Scissors and Glue

If it is difficult for your students to keep glue and scissors at their desks, set up a small table in the classroom and provide several containers of glue, numerous pairs of scissors (sometimes tied to the table), containers of crayons and colored pencils, a stapler, clear tape, and anything else you think students might need to make their Foldables.

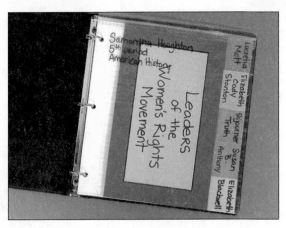

Storing Foldables

There are several ways that students can store their Foldables. They can use grocery bags, plastic bags, or shoeboxes. Students can also punch holes in their Foldables and place them in a three-ring binder. Suggest they place strips of two-inch clear tape along one side and punch three holes through the taped edge.

By keeping all of their Foldables together and organized, students will have created their own portfolio.

HINT: *I found it more convenient to keep student portfolios in my classroom so student work was always available when needed. Giant detergent boxes make good storage containers for portfolios.*

Use This Book as a Creative Resource

Have this book readily available for students to use as an idea reference for projects, discussions, social studies debates, extra credit work, cooperative learning group presentations, and so on. Encourage students to think of their own versions of Foldables to help them learn the material the best way possible.

Using Visuals and Graphics With Foldables

The graphics on pages 6–12 can be used as visual aids for students' Foldables. Students can incorporate them into their journals, notes, projects, and study guides independently. I found that students and teachers were more likely to use graphics if they were available on a classroom computer where they could be selected and printed out as needed. You can also photocopy and distribute the pages that follow for students to trace or cut out for their projects. All these visuals will aid student understanding and retention.

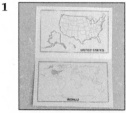

1. Students can mark and label large United States and world maps to show where past and recent events occurred, where a historic person lived and worked, where wars were fought and battles won, where volcanoes are active and inactive, where boundaries of territories or regions existed, and so on.

2. Students can mark and label smaller maps of continents to illustrate more specific locations. For example, when making a *who, what, when, where* Foldable, students can identify exactly where the particular event occurred or where the individual lived.

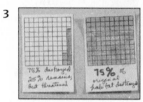

3. Bar graphs, grids, and circle graphs can be used to show changes over time, population distribution, and so on.

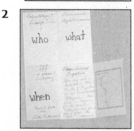

4. Use time lines to record when someone lived or when an event or sequence of events occurred. Use two time lines to compare what was happening in two different areas at the same time.

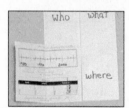

5. Use small picture frames to sketch or name a person, place, or thing.

Africa

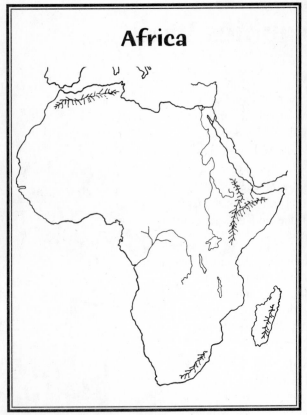

Antarctica

Asia

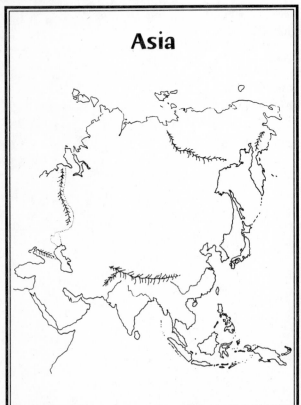

Australia

Europe

North America

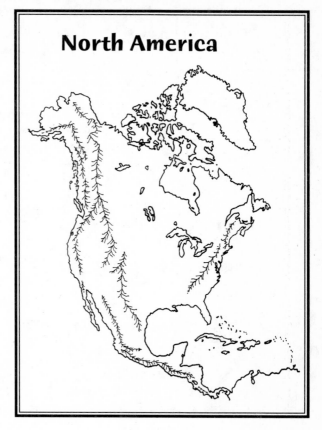

South America

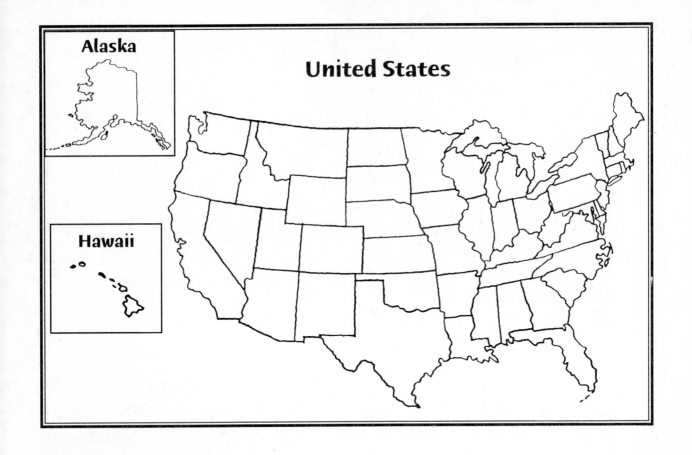

Alaska

Hawaii

United States

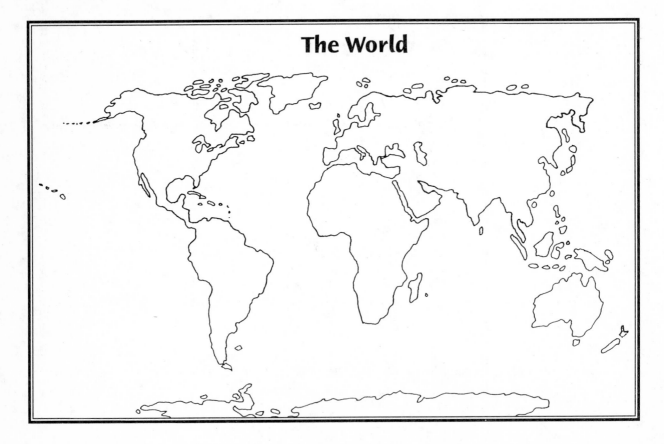

The World

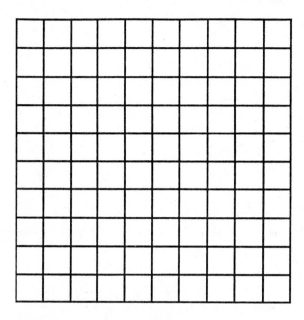

Percentages or bar graph

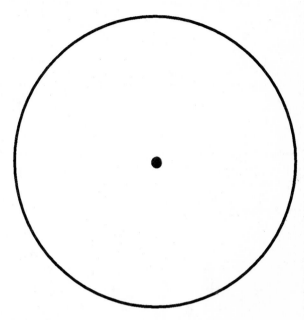

Circle graph

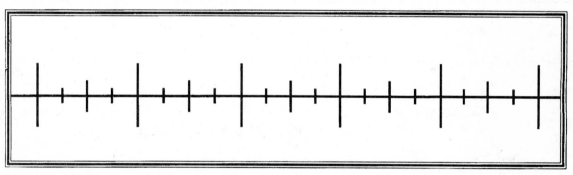

Generic Time Line

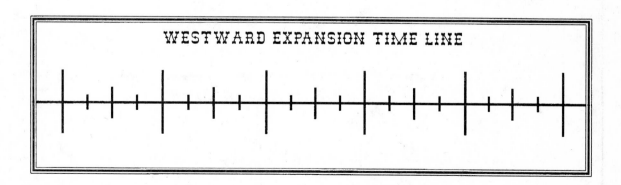

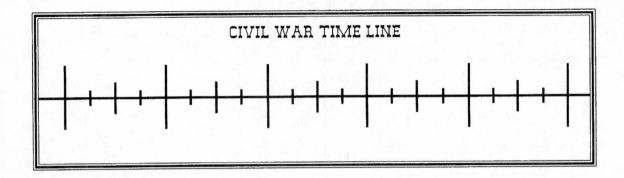

CIVIL WAR TIME LINE

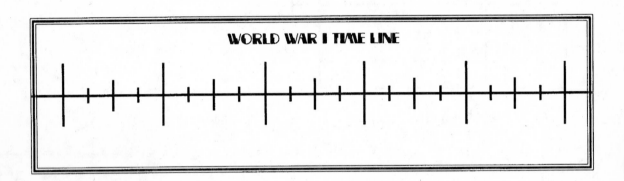

WORLD WAR I TIME LINE

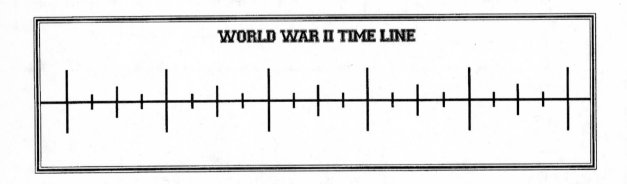

WORLD WAR II TIME LINE

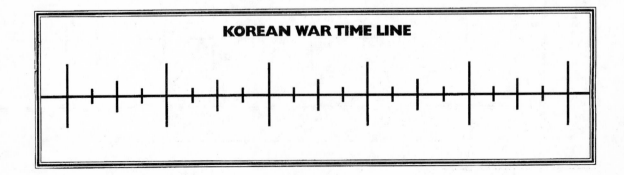

KOREAN WAR TIME LINE

England

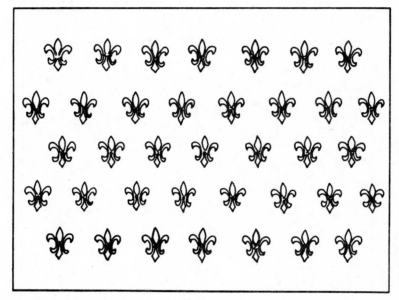

France

Spain

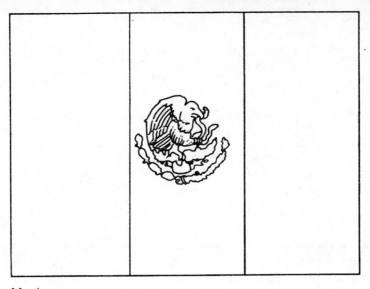

Mexico

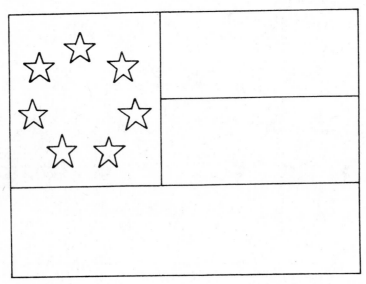

Confederacy

United States of America

Basic Foldables Shapes

The following figures illustrate the basic folds that are referred to throughout the instruction section of this book.

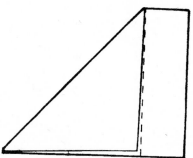

Taco Fold

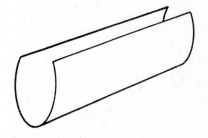

Hamburger Fold

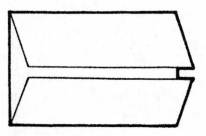

Hot Dog Fold

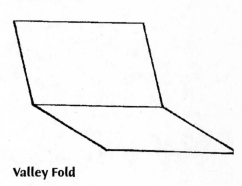

Burrito Fold

Shutter Fold

Valley Fold

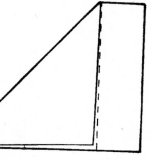

Mountain Fold

Half Book

Fold a sheet of paper in half.

1. This book can be folded vertically like a *hot dog* or . . .

2. . . . it can be folded horizontally like a *hamburger.*

Use this book for descriptive, expository, persuasive, or narrative writing, as well as graphs, diagrams, or charts.

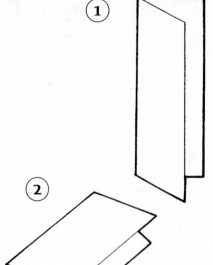

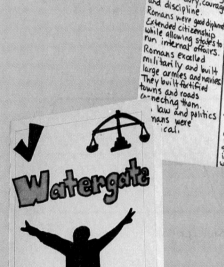

The Seven Continents

Spain in Texas

Folded Book

1. Make a *half-book*. (p. 14)

2. Fold it in half again like a *hamburger*. This makes a ready-made cover and two small pages for information on the inside.

Use photocopied work sheets, Internet printouts, and student-drawn diagrams or maps to make this book. One sheet of paper becomes two activities and two grades.

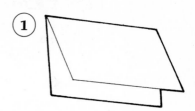

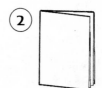

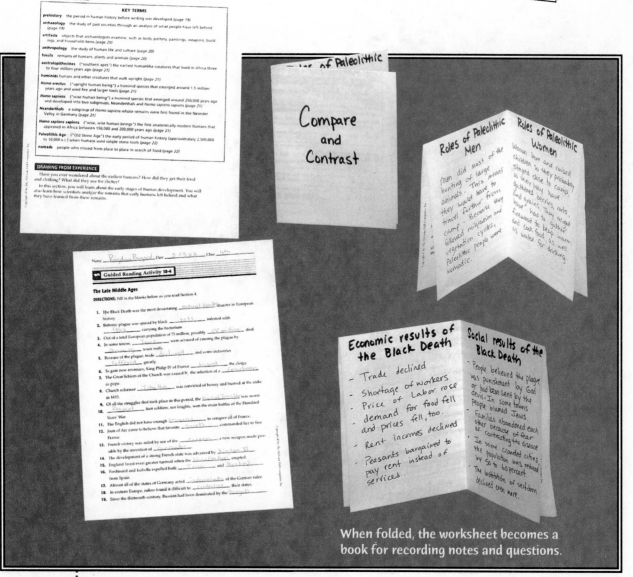

When folded, the worksheet becomes a book for recording notes and questions.

Three-Quarter Book

1. Make a *two-tab book* (p. 18) and raise the left-hand tab.

2. Cut the tab off at the top fold line.

3. A larger book of information can be made by gluing several *three-quarter books* side by side.

Sketch or glue a graphic to the left, write one or more questions on the right, and record answers and information under the right tab.

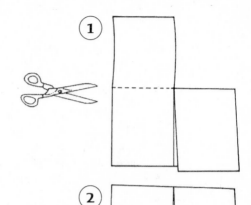

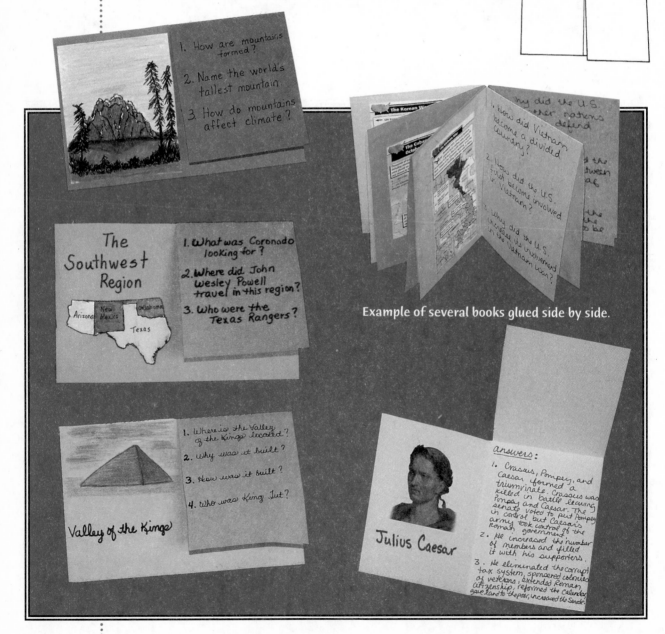

Example of several books glued side by side.

Bound Book

1. Take two sheets of paper and fold them separately like a *hamburger*. Place the papers on top of each other, leaving one-sixteenth of an inch between the *mountain tops*.

2. Mark both folds one inch from the outer edges.

3. On one of the folded sheets, cut slits in the middle to the marked spot on both sides.

4. On the second folded sheet, start at one of the marked spots and cut the fold between the two marks.

5. Take the cut sheet from step 3 and fold it like a *burrito*. Place the *burrito* through the other sheet and then open the *burrito*. Fold the bound pages in half to form an eight-page book.

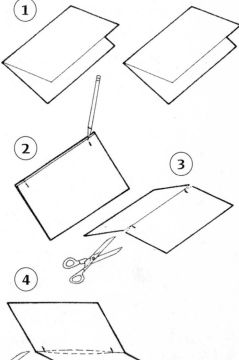

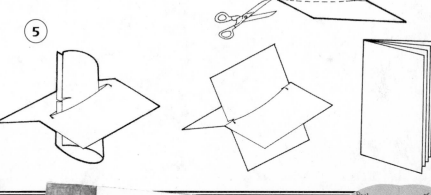

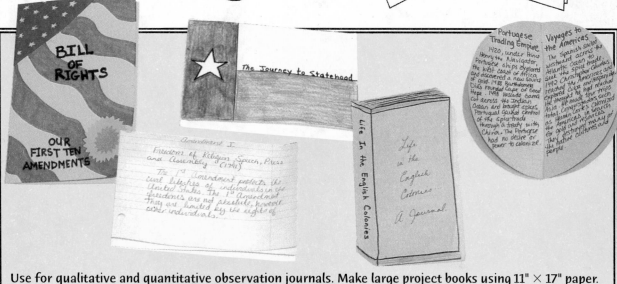

Use for qualitative and quantitative observation journals. Make large project books using 11" × 17" paper.

Two-Tab Book

1. Make a *folded book* (p. 15) and cut up the *valley* of the inside fold toward the *mountain top*. This cut forms two large tabs that can be used for text and illustrations on the front and back.

2. The book can be expanded by making several of these folds and gluing them side by side.

Use this book for learning about two things. For example, use it for comparing and contrasting, determining cause and effect, finding similarities and differences, using Venn diagrams, and so on.

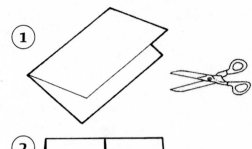

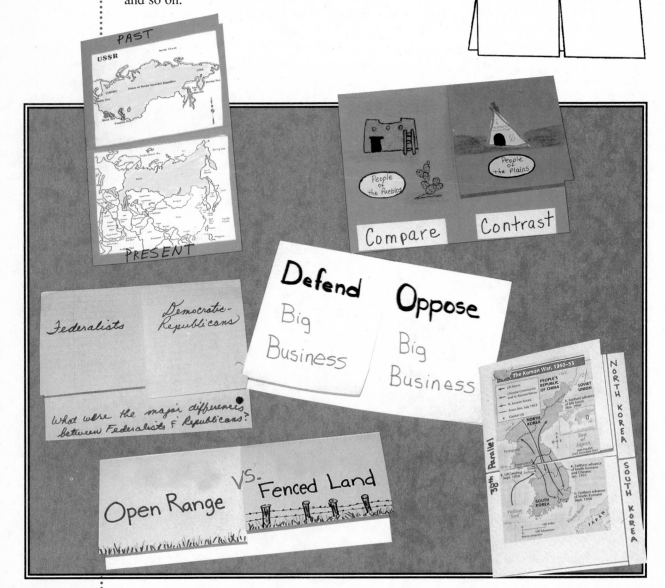

Pocket Book

1. Fold a sheet of paper in half like a *hamburger*.

2. Open the folded paper and fold one of the long sides up two inches to form a pocket. Refold along the *hamburger* fold so that the newly formed pockets are on the inside.

3. Glue the outer edges of the two-inch fold with a small amount of glue.

4. **Optional:** Glue a cover around the *pocket book*.

   Variation: Make a multi-paged booklet by gluing several pockets side by side. Glue a cover around the multi-paged *pocket book.*

Summarize information on note cards or on quarter sheets of notebook paper. Store other foldables, such as *two-tab books,* inside the pockets.

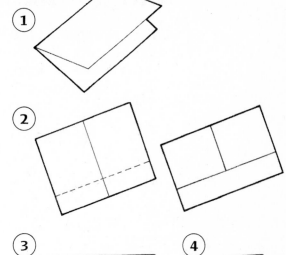

Matchbook

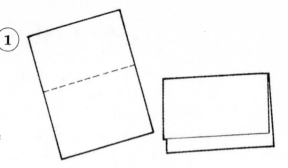

1. Fold a sheet of paper like a *hamburger,* but fold it so that one side is one inch longer than the other side.

2. Fold the one-inch tab over the short side forming a fold like an envelope.

3. Cut the front flap in half toward the *mountain top* to create two flaps.

Use this book to report on one thing, such as a person, place, or thing, or for reporting on two things, such as the cause and effect of Western Expansion.

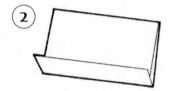

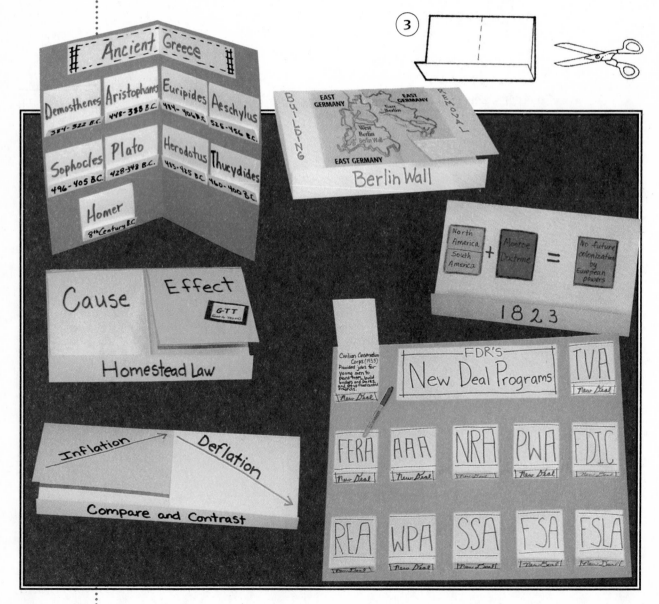

Shutter Fold

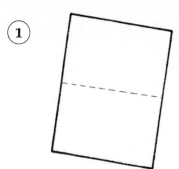

1. Begin as if you were going to make a *hamburger* but instead of creasing the paper, pinch it to show the midpoint.

2. Fold the outer edges of the paper to meet at the pinch, or mid-point, forming a *shutter fold*.

Use this book for comparing two things. Students could also make this foldable with 11" × 17" paper and then glue smaller books—such as the *half book, journal,* and *two-tab book*—inside to create a large project full of student work.

Trifold Book

1. Fold a sheet of paper into thirds.

2. Use this book as is, or cut into shapes. If the trifold is cut, leave plenty of paper on both sides of the designed shape, so the book will open and close in three sections.

Use this book to make charts with three columns or rows, large Venn diagrams, reports on three events or people, or to show and explain the outside and inside of something.

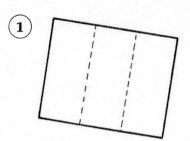

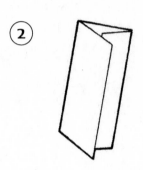

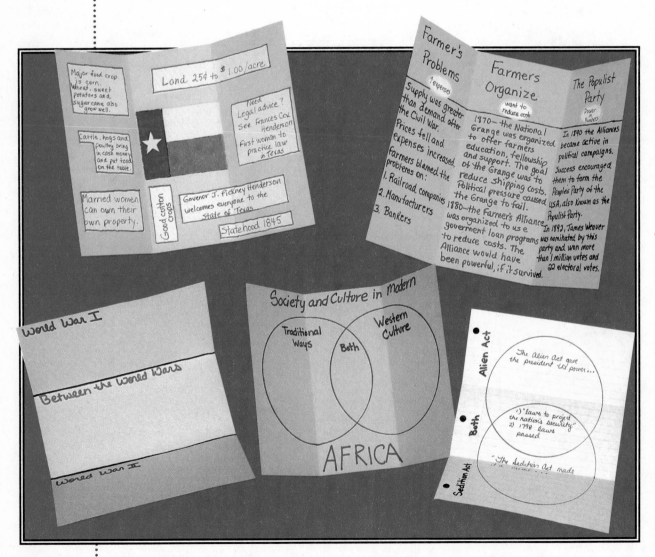

Three-Tab Book

1. Fold a sheet of paper like a *hot dog*.

2. With the paper horizontal, and the fold of the *hot dog* up, fold the right side toward the center, trying to cover one-third of the paper.

   NOTE: *If you fold the right edge over first, the final foldable will open and close like a book.*

3. Fold the left side over the right side to make a book with three folds.

4. Open the folded book. Place your hands between the two thicknesses of paper and cut up the two *valleys* on the top layer only along both folds. This will make three tabs.

Use this book for writing information about three things and for Venn diagrams.

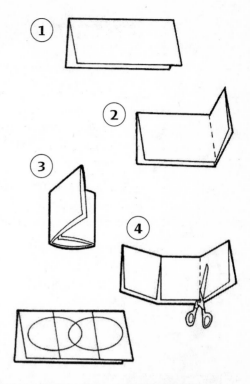

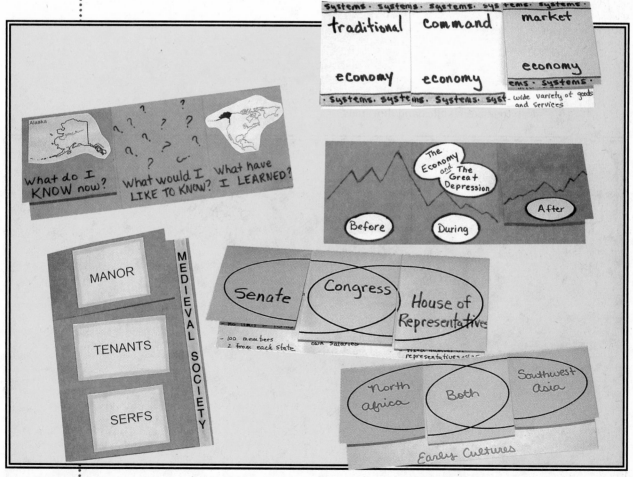

Pyramid Fold

1. Fold a sheet of paper into a *taco,* forming a square. Cut off the leftover piece.

2. Fold the triangle in half. Unfold. The folds will form an X dividing four equal sections.

3. Cut up one fold line and stop at the middle. Draw an X on one tab and label the other three.

4. Fold the X flap under the other flap and glue together. This makes a three-sided pyramid.

Label front sections and write information, notes, thoughts, and questions inside the pyramid on the back of the appropriate tab.

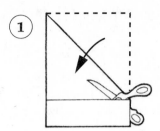

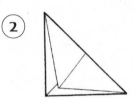
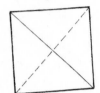

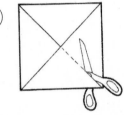

Use to make mobiles and dioramas.

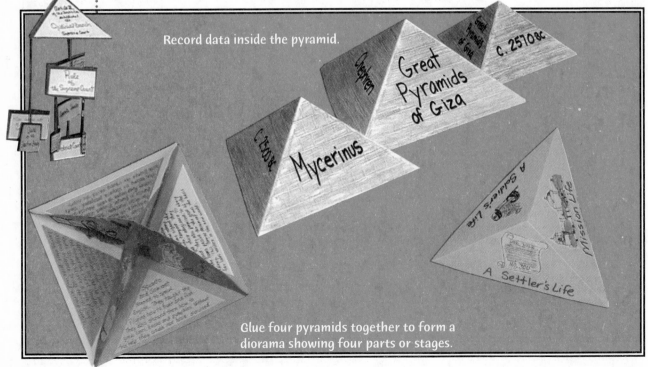

Record data inside the pyramid.

Glue four pyramids together to form a diorama showing four parts or stages.

Layered-Look Book

1. Stack two sheets of paper so that the back sheet is one inch higher than the front sheet.

2. Fold up the bottom edges of the paper to form four tabs. Align the edges so that all of the layers or tabs are the same distance apart.

3. When all tabs are the same size, crease the paper to hold the tabs in place and staple or glue the sheets together.

Glue the sheets together along the *valley* or inner center fold or staple them along the *mountain top*.

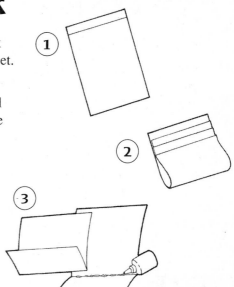

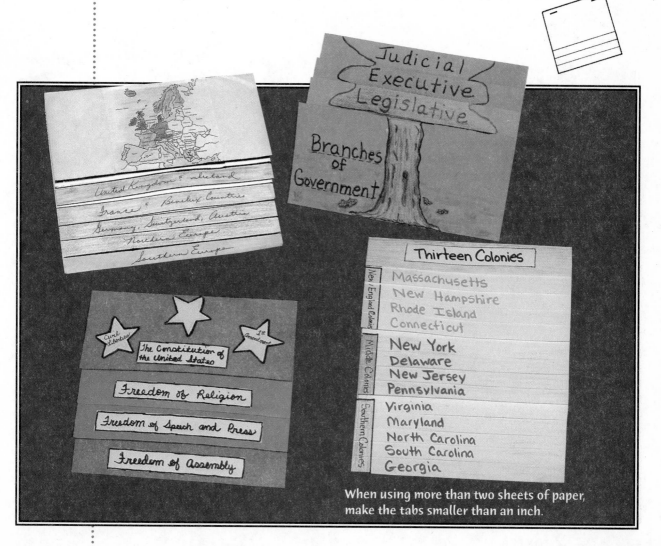

When using more than two sheets of paper, make the tabs smaller than an inch.

Four-Tab Book

1. Fold a sheet of paper in half like a *hot dog*.

2. Fold this long rectangle in half like a *hamburger*.

3. Fold both ends back to touch the *mountain top*.

4. On the side with two *valleys* and one *mountain top,* cut along the three inside fold lines on the front flap to make four tabs.

Use this book for recording information on four things, events, or people.

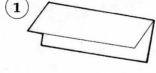

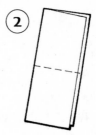

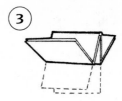

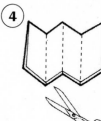

26

Standing Cube

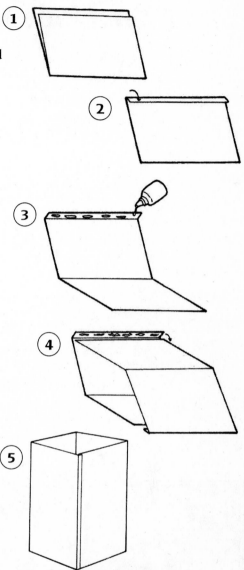

1. Use two sheets of the same size paper. Fold each like a *hamburger.* However, fold one side one-half inch shorter than the other side. This will make a tab that extends out one-half inch on one side.

2. Fold the long side over the short side of both sheets of paper, making tabs.

3. On one of the folded papers, place a small amount of glue along the the small folded tab next to the *valley,* but not in it.

4. Place the non-folded edge of the second sheet of paper square into the *valley* and fold the glue-covered tab over this sheet of paper. Press flat until the glue holds. Repeat with the other side.

5. Allow the glue to dry completely before continuing. After the glue has dried, the cube can be collapsed flat to allow students to work at their desks.

Use the cube for organizing information on four things. Use 11" × 17" paper to make larger project cubes that you can glue other foldables onto for display. Notebook paper, photocopied sheets, magazine pictures, and current events articles can also be displayed on the larger cubes.

These cubes can be stored in plastic bag portfolios by collapsing the cubes to make them flat.

Envelope Fold

1. Fold a sheet of paper into a *taco* forming a square. Cut off the leftover piece.

2. Open the folded *taco* and refold it the opposite way forming another *taco* and an X-fold pattern.

3. Open the *taco fold* and fold the corners toward the center point of the X forming a small square.

4. Trace this square onto another sheet of paper. Cut and glue it to the inside of the envelope. Pictures can be placed under or on top of the tabs.

Use this foldable for organizing information on four things. Use it for "hidden pictures" and current events pictures. Have your classmates raise one tab at a time until they can guess what the picture represents. Number the tabs in the order in which they are to be opened.

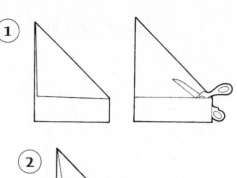

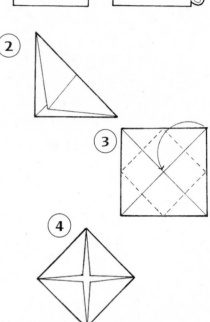

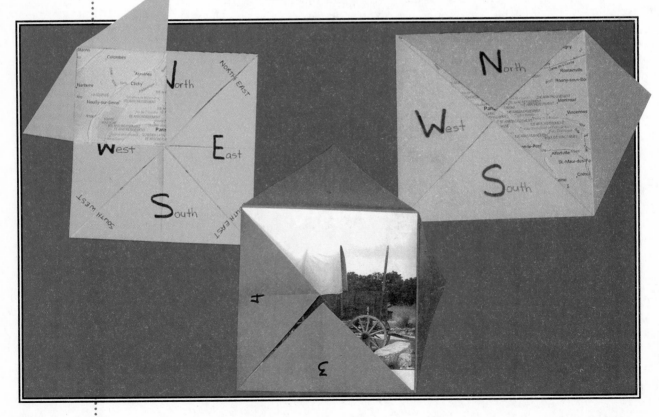

Four-Door Book

1. Make a *shutter fold* (p. 21) using a larger sheet of paper.

2. Fold the *shutter fold* in half like a *hamburger.* Crease well.

3. Open the project and cut along the two inside *valley* folds.

4. These cuts will form four doors on the inside of the project.

Use this book for organizing information on four things. When folded in half like a *hamburger,* a finished *four-door book* can be glued inside a large (11" × 17") *shutter fold* as part of a more inclusive project.

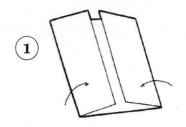

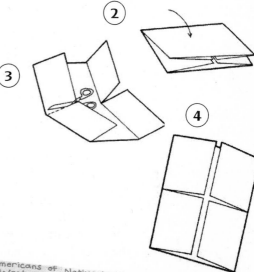

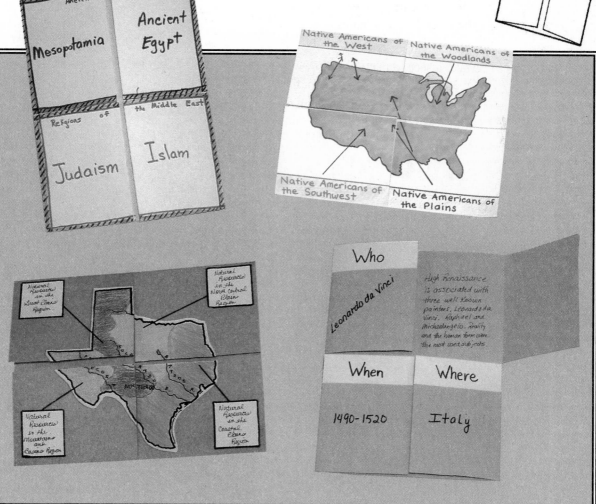

Top-Tab Book

1. Fold a sheet of paper in half like a *hamburger*. Cut the center fold, forming two half sheets.

2. Fold one of the half sheets four times. Begin by folding it in half like a *hamburger,* fold again like a *hamburger,* and finally again like a *hamburger.* This folding has formed your pattern of four rows and four columns, or 16 small squares.

3. Fold two sheets of paper in half like a *hamburger.* Cut the center folds, forming four half sheets.

4. Hold the pattern vertically and place on a half sheet of paper under the pattern. Cut the bottom right hand square out of both sheets. Set this first page aside.

5. Take a second half sheet of paper and place it under the pattern. Cut the first and second right hand squares out of both sheets. Place the second page on top of the first page.

(continued next page)

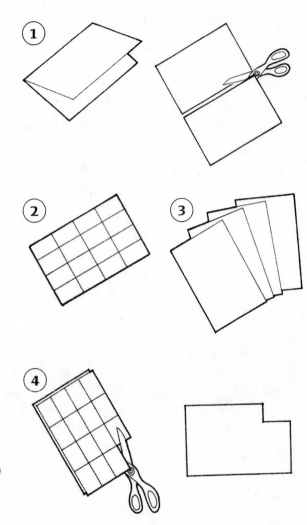

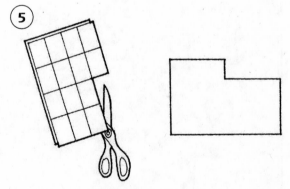

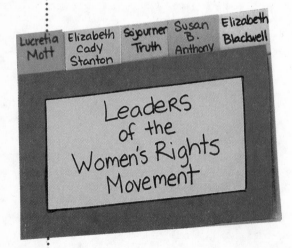

6. Take a third half sheet of paper and place it under the pattern. Cut the first, second, and third right hand squares out of both sheets. Place this third page on top of the second page.

7. Place the fourth, uncut half sheet of paper behind the three cut out sheets, leaving four aligned tabs across the top of the book. Staple several times on the left side. You can also place glue along the left paper edges and stack them together.

8. Cut a final half sheet of paper with no tabs and staple along the left side to form a cover.

Use this foldable to organize several events or characteristics of a person, place, or occurrence.

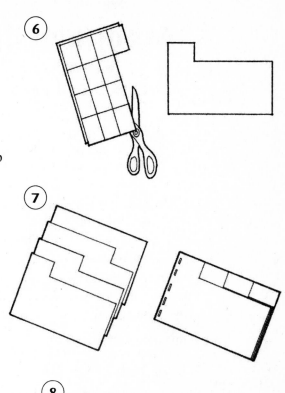

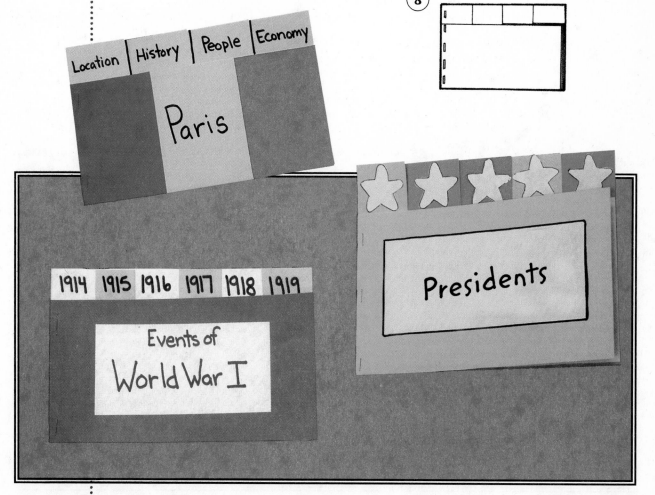

Accordion Book

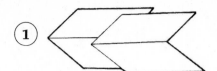

1. Fold two sheets of paper into *hamburgers*.

2. Cut the sheets of paper in half along the fold lines.

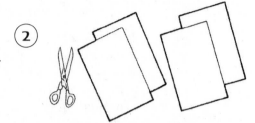

3. Fold each section of paper into *hamburgers*. However, fold one side one-half inch shorter than the other side. This will form a tab that is one-half inch long.

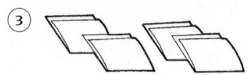

4. Fold this tab forward over the shorter side, and then fold it back from the shorter piece of paper. (In other words, fold it the opposite way.)

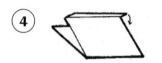

5. Glue together to form an *accordion* by gluing a straight edge of one section into the *valley* of another section.

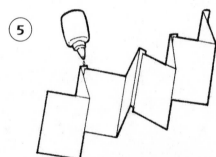

NOTE: *Stand the sections on end to form an* accordion *to help students visualize how to glue them together. See illustration.*

Always place the extra tab at the back of the book so you can add more pages later.

Use this book for time lines, sequencing events or information, biographies, and so on.

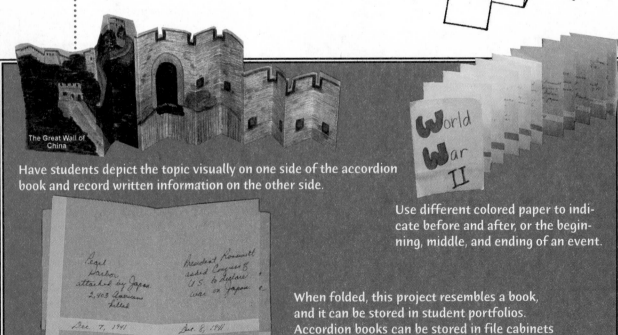

The Great Wall of China

Have students depict the topic visually on one side of the accordion book and record written information on the other side.

World War II

Use different colored paper to indicate before and after, or the beginning, middle, and ending of an event.

Pearl Harbor attacked by Japan 2,403 Americans killed

Dec. 7, 1941

President Roosevelt asked Congress & U.S. to declare war on Japan

Dec. 8, 1941

When folded, this project resembles a book, and it can be stored in student portfolios. Accordion books can be stored in file cabinets for future use.

Pop-Up Book

1. Fold a sheet of paper in half like a *hamburger.*

2. Beginning at the fold, or *mountain top,* cut one or more tabs.

3. Fold the tabs back and forth several times until there is a good fold line formed.

4. Partially open the *hamburger* fold and push the tabs through to the inside.

5. With one small dot of glue, glue figures for the *pop-up book* to the front of each tab. Allow the glue to dry before going on to the next step.

6. Make a cover for the book by folding another sheet of paper in half like a *hamburger.* Place glue around the outside edges of the *pop-up book* and firmly press inside the *hamburger* cover.

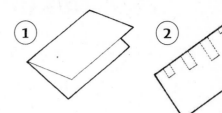

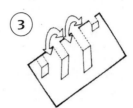

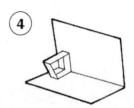

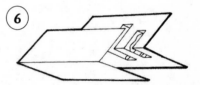

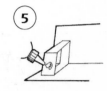

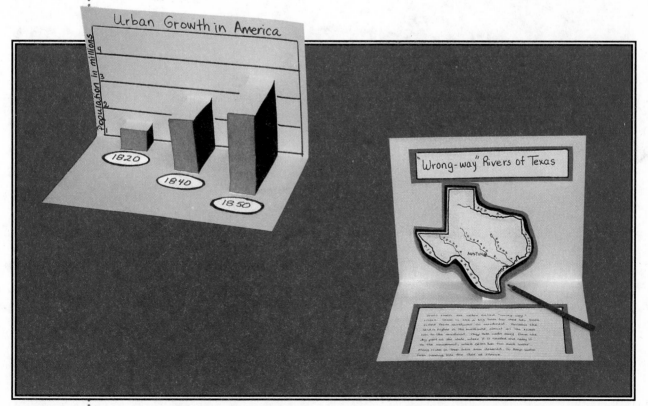

Five-Tab Book

1. Fold a sheet of paper in half like a *hot dog*.

2. Fold the paper so that one-third is exposed and two-thirds are covered.

3. Fold the two-thirds section in half.

4. Fold the one-third section (single thickness) backward to form a fold line.

The paper will be divided into fifths when opened. Use this foldable to organize information about five countries, dates, events, and so on.

①

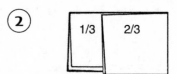

② 1/3 2/3

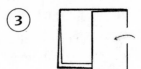

③

④

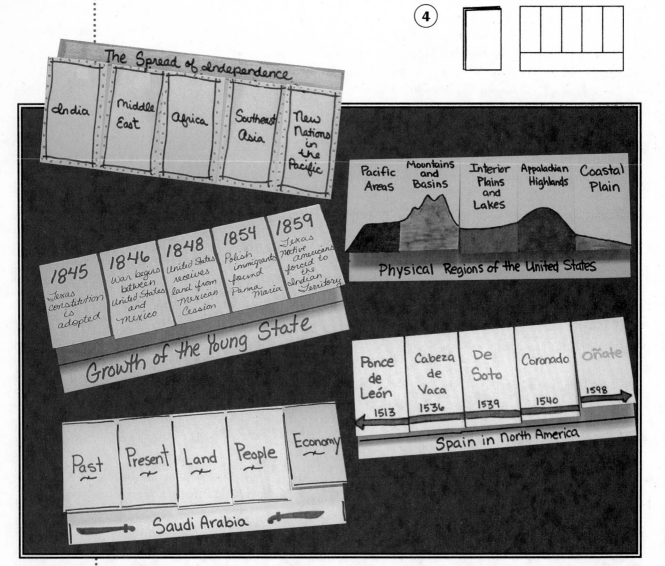

The Spread of Independence

India | Middle East | Africa | Southeast Asia | New Nations in the Pacific

Physical Regions of the United States

Pacific Areas | Mountains and Basins | Interior Plains and Lakes | Appalachian Highlands | Coastal Plain

Growth of the Young State

1845 — Texas constitution is adopted | 1846 — War begins between United States and Mexico | 1848 — United States receives land from Mexican Cession | 1854 — Polish immigrants found Panna Maria | 1859 — Texas Native Americans forced to the Indian Territory

Spain in North America

Ponce de León — 1513 | Cabeza de Vaca — 1536 | De Soto — 1539 | Coronado — 1540 | Oñate — 1598

Past | Present | Land | People | Economy

Saudi Arabia

Folded Table or Chart

1. Fold a sheet of paper into the number of vertical columns needed to make the table or chart.

2. Fold the horizontal rows needed to make the table or chart.

3. Label the rows and columns.

REMEMBER: Tables are organized along vertical and horizontal axes, while charts are organized along one axis, either horizontal or vertical.

Fold the sheet of paper into as many columns or rows that you need for the particular topic.

Table

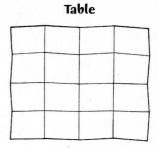

Chart

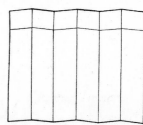

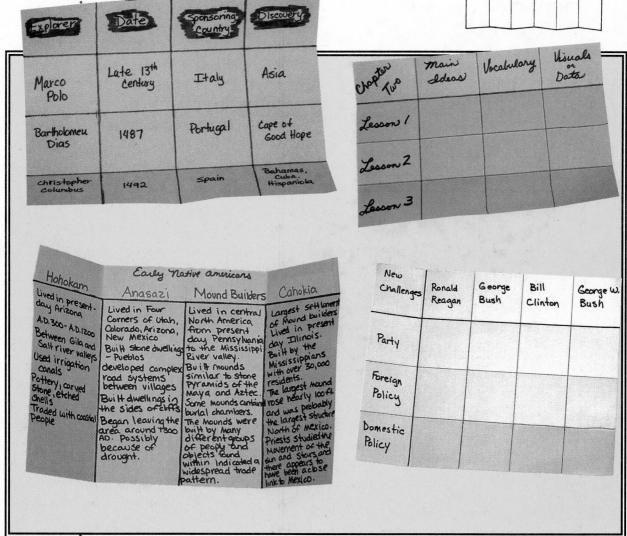

Explorer	Date	Sponsoring Country	Discovery
Marco Polo	Late 13th Century	Italy	Asia
Bartholomeu Dias	1487	Portugal	Cape of Good Hope
christopher columbus	1492	spain	Bahamas, Cuba, Hispaniola

Chapter Two	Main Ideas	Vocabulary	Visuals or Data
Lesson 1			
Lesson 2			
Lesson 3			

Early Native americans

Hohokam	Anasazi	Mound Builders	Cahokia
Lived in present-day Arizona A.D.300 - A.D.1200 Between Gila and Salt river valleys Used irrigation canals Pottery, carved stone, etched shells Traded with coastal People	Lived in Four Corners of Utah, Colorado, Arizona, New Mexico Built Stone dwellings - Pueblos developed complex road systems between villages Built dwellings in the sides of cliffs Began leaving the area around 1300 AD. Possibly because of drought.	Lived in central North America from present day Pennsylvania to the Mississippi River valley. Built mounds similar to stone pyramids of the Maya and Aztec. Some mounds contain burial chambers. The mounds were built by many different groups of people and objects found within indicated a widespread trade pattern.	Largest settlement of Mound builders Lived in present day Illinois. Built by the Mississippians with over 30,000 residents. The largest mound rose nearly 100 ft and was probably the largest structure North of Mexico. Priests studied the movement of the sun and stars and there appears to have been a close link to Mexico.

New Challenges	Ronald Reagan	George Bush	Bill Clinton	George W. Bush
Party				
Foreign Policy				
Domestic Policy				

Folding a Circle Into Tenths

1. Cut a circle out of a sheet of paper. Then fold the circle in half.

2. Fold the half circle so that one-third is exposed and two-thirds are covered.

3. Fold the one-third (single thickness) backward to form a fold line.

4. Fold the two-thirds section in half.

5. The half circle will be divided into fifths. When opened, the circle will be divided into tenths.

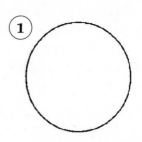

2/3

1/3

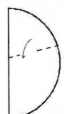

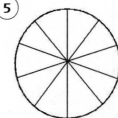

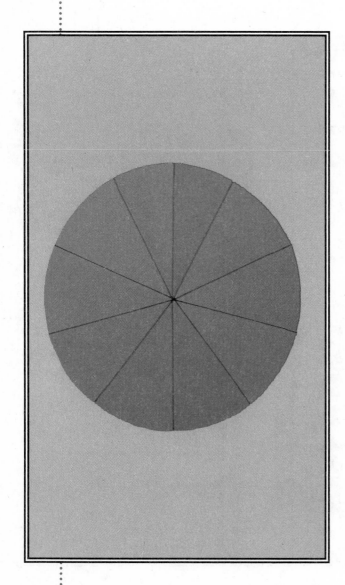

NOTE: *Paper squares and rectangles are folded into tenths the same way. Fold them so that one-third is exposed and two-thirds is covered. Continue with steps 3 and 4.*

Circle Graph

1. Cut out two circles from two sheets of paper.

2. Fold one of the circles in half on each axis, forming fourths. Cut along one of the fold lines (the radius) to the middle of each circle. Flatten the circle.

3. Place the two circles together along the cuts until they overlap completely.

4. Spin one of the circles while holding the other still. Estimate how much of each of the two (or you can add more) circles should be exposed to illustrate percentages or categories of information. Add circles to represent more than two percentages.

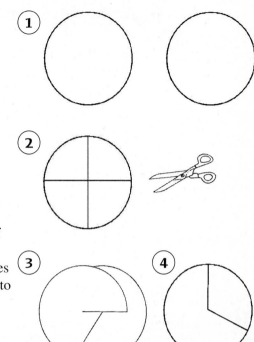

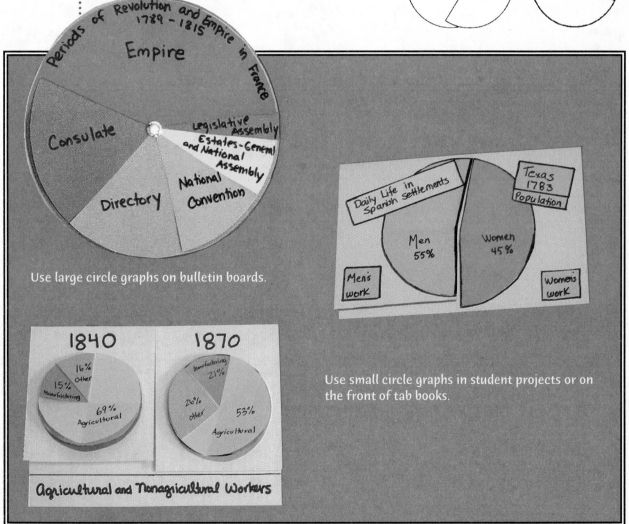

Use large circle graphs on bulletin boards.

Use small circle graphs in student projects or on the front of tab books.

Concept-Map Book

1. Fold a sheet of paper along the long or short axis, leaving a two-inch tab uncovered along the top.

2. Fold in half or in thirds.

3. Unfold and cut along the two or three inside fold lines.

Use this book to write facts about a person, place, or thing under the appropriate tab.

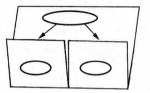

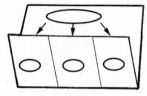

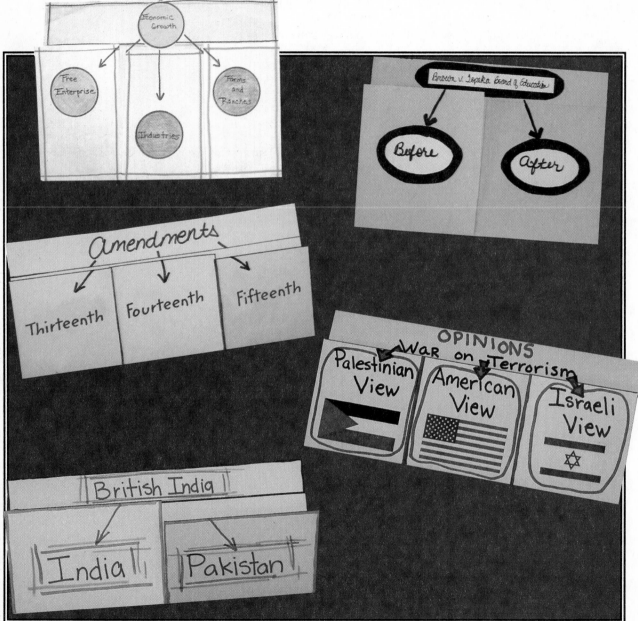

Vocabulary Book

1. Fold a sheet of notebook paper in half like a *hot dog*.

2. On one side, cut every third line. This usually results in ten tabs.

3. Label the tabs. See the illustration below for several uses.

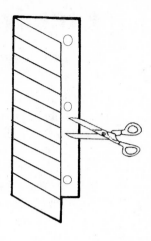

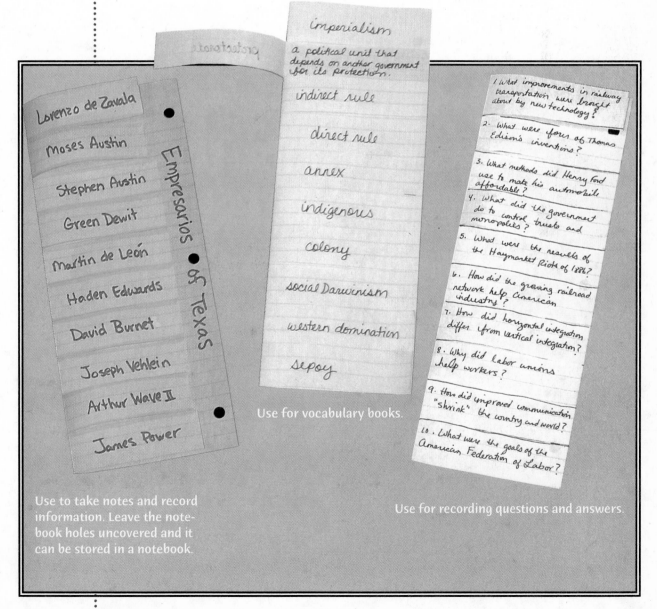

Empresarios • of Texas

Lorenzo de Zavala
Moses Austin
Stephen Austin
Green Dewit
Martin de León
Haden Edwards
David Burnet
Joseph Vehlein
Arthur Wave II
James Power

protectorate

imperialism

a political unit that depends on another government for its protection.

indirect rule

direct rule

annex

indigenous

colony

social Darwinism

western domination

sepoy

Use for vocabulary books.

1. What improvements in railway transportation were brought about by new technology?

2. What were four of Thomas Edison's inventions?

3. What methods did Henry Ford use to make his automobile affordable?

4. What did the government do to control trusts and monopolies?

5. What were the results of the Haymarket Riots of 1886?

6. How did the growing railroad network help American industry?

7. How did horizontal integration differ from vertical integration?

8. Why did labor unions help workers?

9. How did improved communication "shrink" the country and world?

10. What were the goals of the American Federation of Labor?

Use to take notes and record information. Leave the notebook holes uncovered and it can be stored in a notebook.

Use for recording questions and answers.

Four-Door Diorama

1. Make a *four-door book* out of a *shutter fold* (p. 21).

2. Fold the two inside corners back to the outer edges *(mountains)* of the *shutter fold*. This will result in two *tacos* that will make the *four-door book* look like it has a shirt collar. Do the same thing to the bottom of the *four-door book*. When finished, four small triangular *tacos* have been made.

3. Form a 90-degree angle and overlap the folded triangles to make a display case that doesn't use staples or glue. (It can be collapsed for storage.)

4. Or, as illustrated, cut off all four triangles, or *tacos*. Staple or glue the sides.

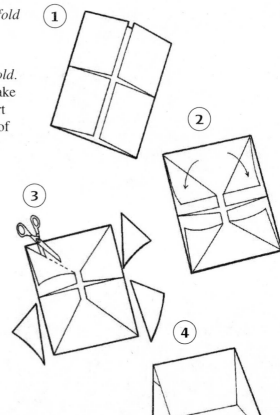

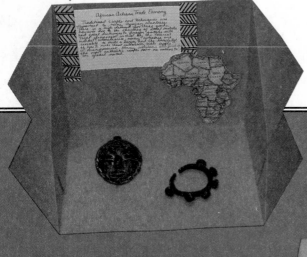

Use 11" × 17" paper to make a large display case.

Use poster board to make giant display cases.

Place display cases next to each other to compare and contrast or to sequence events or data.

Picture Frame Book

1. Fold a sheet of paper in half like a *hamburger.*

2. Open the *hamburger* and gently roll one side of the *hamburger* toward the *valley.* Try not to crease the roll.

3. Cut a rectangle out of the middle of the rolled side of the paper leaving a half-inch border, forming a frame.

4. Fold another sheet of paper in half like a *hamburger.* Apply glue to the inside border of the picture frame and place the folded, uncut sheet of paper inside.

Use this book to feature a person, place, or thing. Inside the picture frames, glue photographs, magazine pictures, computer-generated graphs, or have students sketch pictures. This book has three inside pages for writing and recording notes.

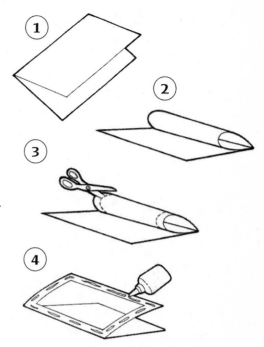

Display Case

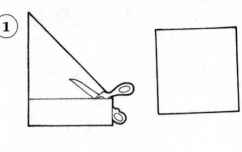

1. Make a *taco* fold and cut off the leftover piece. This will result in a square.

2. Fold the square into a *shutter fold*.

3. Unfold and fold the square into another *shutter fold* perpendicular to the direction of the first. This will form a small square at each of the four corners of the sheet of paper.

4. As illustrated, cut along two fold lines on opposite sides of the large square.

5. Collapse the sides in and glue the tabs to form an open box.

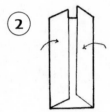
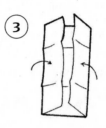
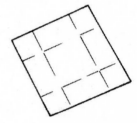

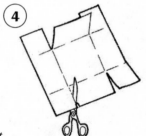

How to Make a Lid

Fold another open-sided box using a square of paper one-half inch larger than the square used to make the first box. This will make a lid that fits snugly over the display box. *Example:* If the base is made out of an $8\frac{1}{2}$" paper square, make the lid out of a 9" square.

Cut a hole out of the lid and cover the opening with a cut piece of acetate used on overhead projectors. Heavy, clear plastic wrap or scraps from a laminating machine will also work. Secure the clear plastic sheet to the inside of the lid with glue or tape.

NOTE: *You can place polystyrene foam or quilt batting in the boxes to display objects. Glue the boxes onto a sheet of cardboard to make them strong enough to display heavy objects.*

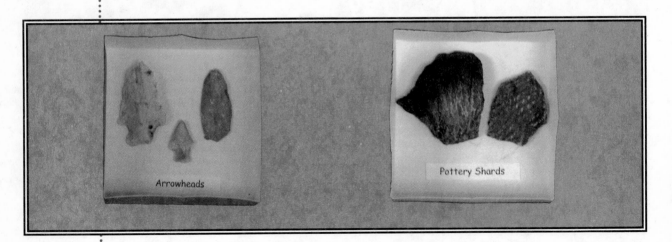

Arrowheads

Pottery Shards

Billboard Project

1. Fold all pieces of the same size of paper in half like *hamburgers*.

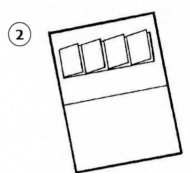

2. Place a line of glue at the top and bottom of one side of each folded billboard section and glue them side by side on a larger sheet of paper or poster board. If glued correctly, all doors will open from right to left.

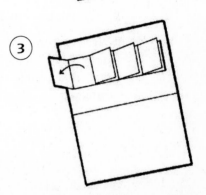

3. Pictures, dates, words, and so on, go on the front of each billboard section. When opened, writing or drawings can be seen on the inside left of each section. The base, or the part glued to the background, is perfect for more in-depth information or definitions.

Use for time lines or for sequencing information, such as events in a war, presidents of the United States, or ratification of states.

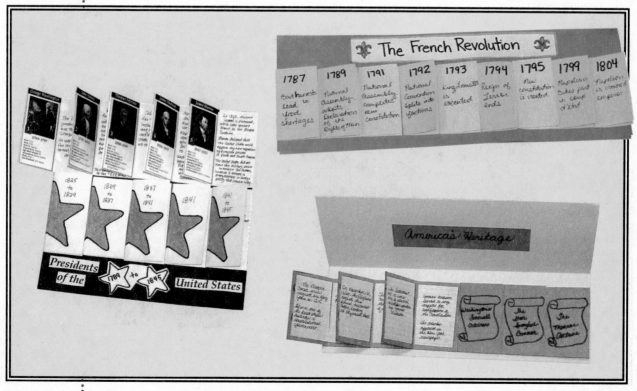

Project Board With Tabs

1. Draw a large illustration, a series of small illustrations, or write on the front of a sheet of paper.

2. Pinch and slightly fold the sheet of paper at the point where a tab is desired on the illustrated sheet of paper. Cut into the paper on the fold. Cut straight in, then cut up to form an "L." When the paper is unfolded, it will form a tab with an illustration on the front.

3. After all tabs have been cut, glue this front sheet onto a second sheet of paper. Place glue around all four edges and in the middle, away from tabs.

Write or draw under the tabs. If the project is made as a bulletin board using butcher paper, tape or glue smaller sheets of paper under the tabs.

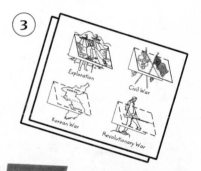

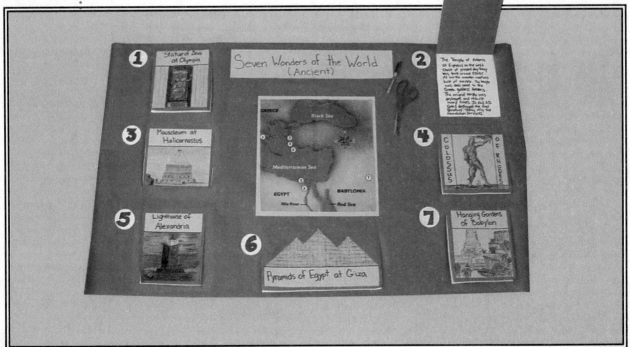

Sentence Strips

1. Take two sheets of paper and fold then into *hamburgers*. Cut along the fold lines making four half sheets. (Use as many half sheets as necessary for additional pages to your book.)

2. Fold each sheet in half like a *hot dog*.

3. Place the folds side by side and staple them together on the left side.

4. One inch from the stapled edge, cut the front page of each folded section up to the *mountain top*. These cuts form flaps that can be raised and lowered.

To make a half-cover, use a sheet of construction paper one inch longer than the book. Glue the back of the last sheet to the construction paper strip leaving one inch on the left side to fold over and cover the original staples. Staple this half-cover in place.

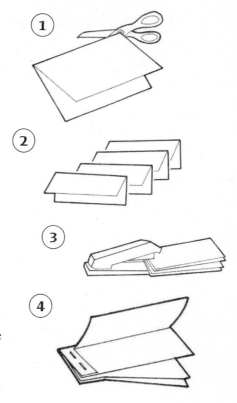

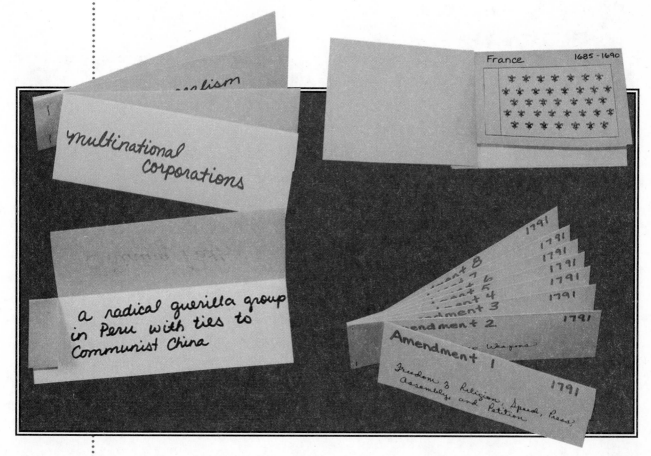

Sentence-Strip Holder

1. Fold a sheet of paper in half like a *hamburger*.

2. Open the *hamburger* and fold the two outer edges toward the *valley*. This forms a *shutter fold*.

3. Fold one of the inside edges of the shutter back to the outside fold. This fold forms a floppy L-tab.

4. Glue the floppy L-tab down to the base so that it forms a strong, straight L-tab.

5. Glue the other shutter side to the front of this L-tab. This forms a tent that is the backboard for the flashcards or student work to be displayed.

6. Fold the edge of the L-tab up one-quarter to one-half inch to form a lip that will keep the student work from slipping off the holder.

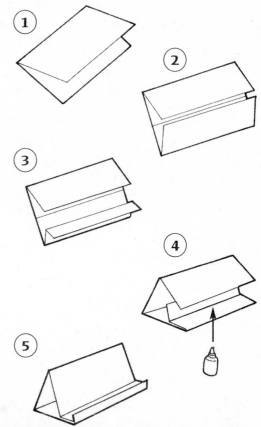

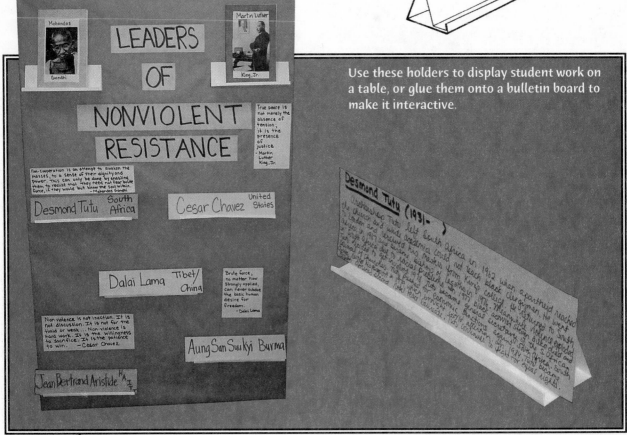

Use these holders to display student work on a table, or glue them onto a bulletin board to make it interactive.

Forward-Backward Book

1. Stack three or more sheets of paper. On the top sheet, trace a large circle.

2. With the papers still stacked, cut out the circles.

3. Staple the paper circles together along the left-hand side to create a circular booklet.

4. Label the cover and takes notes on the pages that open to the right.

5. Turn the book upside down and label the back. Takes notes on the pages that open to the right.

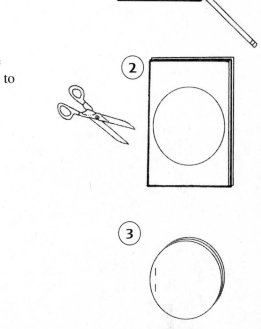

Front

Back

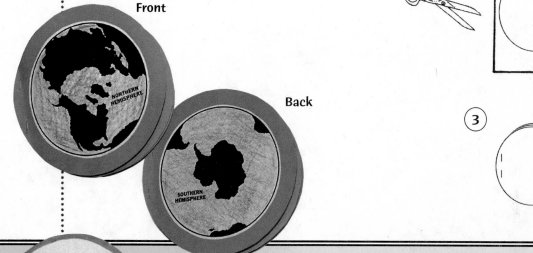

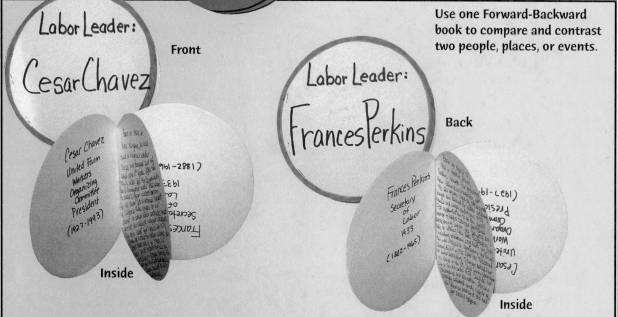

Front

Back

Inside

Inside

Use one Forward-Backward book to compare and contrast two people, places, or events.

Three-Pocket Book

1. Fold a horizontal sheet of paper (11" × 17") into thirds.

2. Fold the bottom edge up two inches and crease well. Glue the outer edges of the two-inch tab to create three pockets.

3. Label each pocket. Use these pockets to hold notes taken on index cards or quarter sheets of paper.

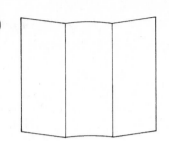

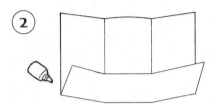

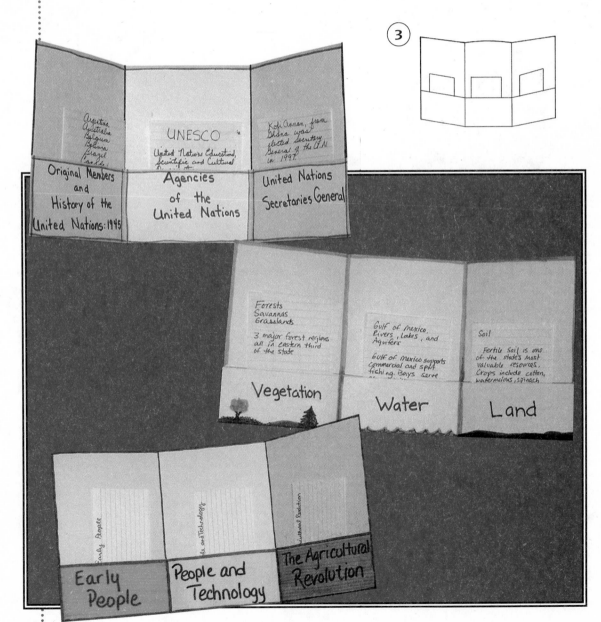

Chapter Activities for

OUR WORLD TODAY

People, Places, and Issues

The pages that follow contain chapter-specific Foldables activities to use with *Our World Today: People, Places, and Issues*. Included are a Chapter Summary, a reproduction of the Foldables Study Organizer that appears on each chapter opener in the textbook, and a Follow-Up Foldables Activity. Use the Follow-Up Activity after students have studied each chapter. Students are asked to use the Foldables they have created and completed during the study of each chapter to review important chapter concepts and prepare for the chapter test.

Alternative Foldables activities are also included for every chapter. Use these activities during the study of each chapter or as chapter review activities. The Student Study Tip provides reading, writing, and test-taking strategies that you can share with your students throughout the course.

Chapter 1	Our Social World	Chapter 13	Russia and Its Neighbors
Chapter 2	Earth Patterns	Chapter 14	Russia—Past and Present
Chapter 3	North Africa and Southwest Asia—Early Cultures	Chapter 15	East and Central Africa
		Chapter 16	West Africa
Chapter 4	North Africa and Southwest Asia Today	Chapter 17	South Africa and Its Neighbors
		Chapter 18	Canada
Chapter 5	South Asia	Chapter 19	The United States
Chapter 6	China and Its Neighbors	Chapter 20	Mexico
Chapter 7	Japan and the Koreas	Chapter 21	Central America and the West Indies
Chapter 8	Southeast Asia		
Chapter 9	Europe—Early History	Chapter 22	Brazil and Its Neighbors
Chapter 10	Europe—Modern History	Chapter 23	The Andean Countries
Chapter 11	Western Europe Today	Chapter 24	Australia and New Zealand
Chapter 12	Eastern Europe Today	Chapter 25	Oceania and Antarctica

Chapter-Specific

FOLDABLES

Our Social World

CHAPTER SUMMARY

Modern technology has helped to bring the world's diverse peoples together. It is important to understand the differences and similarities between ethnic groups and one way to do this is to study their histories. Culture is the way of life of people who share similar beliefs and customs. Those who share the same culture usually live close to others who have similar beliefs and like the same foods, music, and clothing. More and more people are moving from one place to another to look for better opportunities and freedoms.

CHAPTER PREVIEW

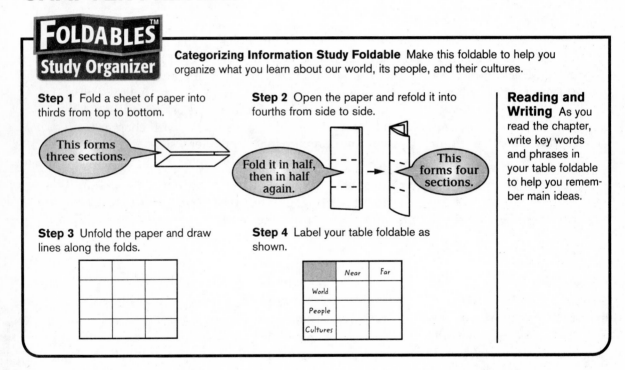

FOLDABLES™
Study Organizer

Categorizing Information Study Foldable Make this foldable to help you organize what you learn about our world, its people, and their cultures.

Step 1 Fold a sheet of paper into thirds from top to bottom.

This forms three sections.

Step 2 Open the paper and refold it into fourths from side to side.

Fold it in half, then in half again.

This forms four sections.

Reading and Writing As you read the chapter, write key words and phrases in your table foldable to help you remember main ideas.

Step 3 Unfold the paper and draw lines along the folds.

Step 4 Label your table foldable as shown.

	Near	Far
World		
People		
Cultures		

CHAPTER REVIEW

Foldables Follow-Up Activity

Once students have completed their foldables, ask them to think about their own cultural background and how it is represented in society. Ask them to research what things in our society are unique to their culture. For example, there are many river and town names in Spanish, and many were named by Native Americans. It is also believed that doughnuts originated in Germany or the Netherlands. Encourage students to share their foldables with others.

Alternative Activities for Chapter 1

COMPARING

Have students label the columns of their foldables with the words *Communication* and *Transportation*. Then have them write *Before 1920* and *After 1920* in the rows. Ask students to compare how inventions have changed communication and transportation before 1920 and after 1920. Have students share this information with the class.

The World's Technology	Communication	Transportation
Before 1920		
After 1920		

My Community		
Majority Groups	Minority Groups	Ethnic Groups

IDENTIFYING

Students should write *Majority Groups*, *Minority Groups*, and *Ethnic Groups* at the top of their foldables, and then write a definition for each using the information in the chapter. Ask them to think about the different groups that live in their community and identify two unique characteristics about each group under the appropriate heading.

Student Study Tip

To help students write a well-developed essay, remind them that the essay's first paragraph should contain a topic sentence that states the main idea. Throughout the essay, students should use examples, supporting details, and transitional words or phrases such as *therefore, as a result,* and *in addition* to support the main idea.

Chapter 1 FOLDABLES

Earth Patterns

CHAPTER SUMMARY

Geographers use various tools to understand the world. They not only study the earth's land, water, air, and animals, but look at how humans interact with their environment. Geographers use maps, globes, photographs, the Global Positioning System, and geographic information systems to study the earth. The variety of Earth's land-forms affects how people live. The actions people take can have serious effects on the environment. For example, it is important to manage water resources because the earth's freshwater supply is limited.

CHAPTER PREVIEW

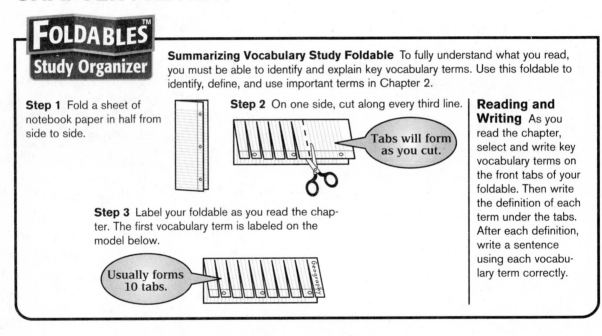

FOLDABLES™
Study Organizer

Summarizing Vocabulary Study Foldable To fully understand what you read, you must be able to identify and explain key vocabulary terms. Use this foldable to identify, define, and use important terms in Chapter 2.

Step 1 Fold a sheet of notebook paper in half from side to side.

Step 2 On one side, cut along every third line.

Tabs will form as you cut.

Step 3 Label your foldable as you read the chapter. The first vocabulary term is labeled on the model below.

Usually forms 10 tabs.

Geography

Reading and Writing As you read the chapter, select and write key vocabulary terms on the front tabs of your foldable. Then write the definition of each term under the tabs. After each definition, write a sentence using each vocabulary term correctly.

CHAPTER REVIEW

Foldables Follow-Up Activity

Once students have created their foldables, have them write a poem, series of journal entries, or short story using most of the vocabulary words on their foldables. For example, they could write a story about a geographer's typical day or a few journal entries on a sight-seeing trip they might take to learn about different landforms. Tell students that they should not include sentences that have already been written on their foldables.

Alternative Activities for Chapter 2

DESCRIBING

Have students write 10 bodies of water on their foldable tabs, and then describe them underneath the tabs. Remind students that rivers, lakes, and oceans are all bodies of water. Then have students locate the bodies of water on a map or globe. For a more challenging activity, suggest that students think of and research 10 locations around the world that have different physical characteristics like hills, mountains, plateaus, plains, and canyons.

IDENTIFYING OPTIONS

Ask students to list 10 ways in which people can help protect the environment. They can use information from the chapter or list their own ideas. On the inside of their foldables, ask students to write ways in which they can personally help protect the environment. Encourage students to volunteer with community organizations that help protect the environment.

Student Study Tip

Share the following tips with your students about taking notes from their textbooks. First, they should read one section without taking notes to focus on understanding the material. Second, they should locate the main ideas and restate them in their own words. Finally, they should write the paraphrased ideas in their notebooks and review them daily.

Chapter 2 **FOLDABLES**

North Africa and Southwest Asia–Early Cultures

CHAPTER SUMMARY

Learning how past cultures lived helps us better understand our own culture. One of the first civilizations developed in the Fertile Crescent between the Tigris and Euphrates Rivers. Farming, writing, and a system of government were first established in Mesopotamia, Sumer, and Phoenicia. Three of the world's monotheistic religions—Judaism, Christianity, and Islam—all developed in Southwest Asia. Judaism is the oldest of the three religions and was first practiced by Hebrews. Christianity is the world's largest religion and Islam is the second largest religion. The followers of Islam are called Muslims, or Moslems.

CHAPTER PREVIEW

Compare-Contrast Study Foldable Make and use this foldable to help you determine how Mesopotamia and ancient Egypt were similar and different.

Step 1 Fold a sheet of paper from side to side, leaving a 2-inch tab uncovered along the side.

Fold it so the left edge lies 2 inches from the right edge.

Step 2 Turn the paper and fold it into thirds.

Reading and Writing As you read the chapter, write what you learn about these ancient civilizations under the tabs. Be sure to list similarities and differences under the appropriate tabs.

Step 3 Unfold and cut along the two inside fold lines.

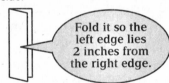

Cut along the two folds on the front flap to make 3 tabs.

Step 4 Label your foldable as shown.

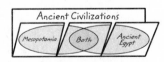
Ancient Civilizations
Mesopotamia   Both   Ancient Egypt

CHAPTER REVIEW

Foldables Follow-Up Activity

Once students have created their foldables, organize students into small groups. Have them discuss the similarities and differences in the ancient civilizations compared to today's. Then have them compile the results in a one-page report. Students should write an introductory paragraph, a paragraph about similarities, a paragraph about differences, and a conclusion.

Alternative Activities for Chapter 3

COMPARE AND CONTRAST

Have students compare and contrast the people of Mesopotamia and Ancient Egypt. Students should draw a Venn diagram on their foldables and write *Phoenicians* and *Egyptians* in the circles. Have students choose one interesting fact about each group to research further. For example, students may choose to do research about how the Egyptian people built pyramids. Have students present their findings to the class.

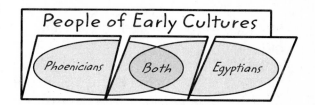

People of Early Cultures — Phoenicians / Both / Egyptians

Religions — Christianity / Both / Islam

MAKING GENERALIZATIONS

Using the information in the text, have students make a foldable to compare and contrast Christianity and Islam. Ask students why they think there are different religions and why they think geographic location sometimes determines which religion people follow. Then discuss the different religious holidays with students.

Student Study Tip

As students are learning the chapter, remind them that time lines are effective study guides. Time lines should include events in the order in which they occurred with a brief description about each event. For this chapter in particular, teach students how historians use "B.C." Time lines enhance learning as students see the development of patterns over time and how events occurred chronologically.

Chapter 3 FOLDABLES

North Africa and Southwest Asia Today

CHAPTER SUMMARY

North Africa and Southwest Asia are considered the "crossroads of the world" because of their location near Europe and Asia. North Africa includes Egypt, Libya, Tunisia, Algeria, and Morocco. North Africa's desert landscape has shaped the people and culture for many centuries, as has the Islamic religion. Turkey and Israel have strong ties to Europe and the United States. About 80 percent of Israel's population are Jews. Syria, Lebanon, Jordan, and Saudi Arabia have Arab populations but different economies and forms of government. Saudi Arabia is the world's leading oil producer. Iran, Iraq, and Afghanistan have recently fought wars and undergone major political changes.

CHAPTER PREVIEW

FOLDABLES™
Study Organizer

Categorizing Information Study Foldable Asking yourself questions while reading material helps you to focus on what you are reading. Make this foldable to help you ask and answer questions about the people and places in North Africa and Southwest Asia.

Step 1 Fold a sheet of paper in half from side to side, leaving a $\frac{1}{2}$ inch tab along the side.

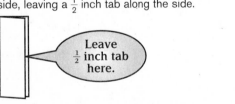

Leave $\frac{1}{2}$ inch tab here.

Step 2 Turn the paper and fold it into fourths.

Fold in half, then fold in half again.

Reading and Writing As you read, ask yourself questions about these countries. Write your questions and answers under each appropriate tab.

Step 3 Unfold and cut up along the three fold lines.

Make four tabs.

Step 4 Label as shown.

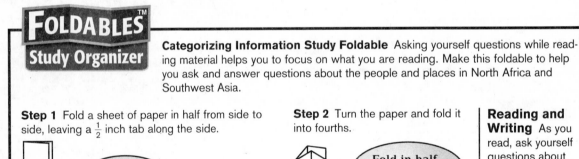

Egypt, Libya, the Maghreb | Turkey, Israel | Syria, Lebanon, Jordan, Arabia | Iraq, Iran, Afghanistan

CHAPTER REVIEW

Foldables Follow-Up Activity

Organize students into pairs. Have one student ask his or her partner a question that is written on the foldable tab. The other student should answer the question by identifying the correct country. Students should take turns asking and answering each other's questions.

Alternative Activities for Chapter 4

DESCRIBING

Have students research information about the landforms, government, economy, and religion of a country described in the chapter and write it under the appropriate tab on their foldables. Then have students who chose the same country form a small group to compare and contrast the similarities and differences in the information that they listed.

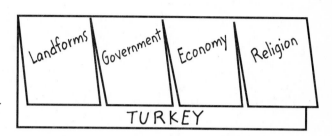

ORGANIZING

Have students identify four countries described in the chapter and write the country's names on the foldable tabs. Students should research newspapers and the Internet to find six historical or cultural facts about each country and write this information under the appropriate tab. Students may also want to draw each country's flag under the tab using colored markers or pencils. Have students work in small groups to discuss what they learned about the countries using the information on their foldables.

Student Study Tip

After students have read the chapter, have them review any new vocabulary terms. Students should begin at Section 1 and identify each new vocabulary term and describe it in their own words. If students have difficulty identifying the term's meaning, have them read the definition aloud. Then have students summarize the definition in their own words.

Chapter 4 FOLDABLES

South Asia

CHAPTER SUMMARY

The countries of South Asia have diverse populations, languages, cultures, and religions. India is the largest country in South Asia in size and population, with more than 1 billion people. India's economy is based on both farming and industry, but it is trying to further develop its resources to meet the needs of a rapidly growing population. Other countries of South Asia include Pakistan, Bangladesh, Nepal, Bhutan, and the island country of Sri Lanka. Farming is an important economic activity for these countries.

CHAPTER PREVIEW

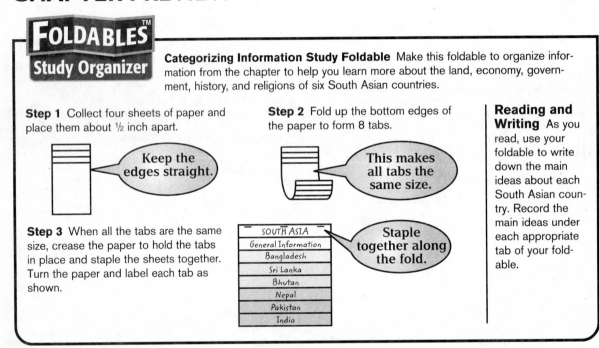

FOLDABLES™
Study Organizer

Categorizing Information Study Foldable Make this foldable to organize information from the chapter to help you learn more about the land, economy, government, history, and religions of six South Asian countries.

Step 1 Collect four sheets of paper and place them about ½ inch apart.

Keep the edges straight.

Step 2 Fold up the bottom edges of the paper to form 8 tabs.

This makes all tabs the same size.

Step 3 When all the tabs are the same size, crease the paper to hold the tabs in place and staple the sheets together. Turn the paper and label each tab as shown.

SOUTH ASIA
General Information
Bangladesh
Sri Lanka
Bhutan
Nepal
Pakistan
India

Staple together along the fold.

Reading and Writing As you read, use your foldable to write down the main ideas about each South Asian country. Record the main ideas under each appropriate tab of your foldable.

CHAPTER REVIEW

Foldables Follow-Up Activity

Once students have completed their foldables, write each country's name on the board. Call on students to share the main ideas they placed on their foldables, and write these on the board for the class. When all main ideas have been identified, have students discuss the similarities and differences among the countries of South Asia. Then erase the country's names on the board, and ask for volunteers to correctly identify the country from the set of characteristics.

Alternative Activities for Chapter 5

CATEGORIZING

Have students use two sheets of paper to create this foldable. Ask students to choose a country from the chapter, and then write historical and present-day facts about the country's land, people, and economy on the foldable tabs. After students have created their foldables, have them research the country that they chose on the Internet or at the library to add more information to their foldables. As a class, discuss the students' findings.

PAKISTAN: Past and Present
land
people
economy

Leaders of India:
Indira Gandhi
Mohandas Gandhi
Jawaharlal Nehru

IDENTIFYING

Have students write the following on their foldables: *Indira Gandhi, Mohandas Gandhi,* and *Jawaharlal Nehru.* Using information from the library or the Internet, have students write facts about the leader under the appropriate tab. Ask volunteers to read a fact from his or her foldable while the other students try to guess which leader is being described.

Student Study Tip

Have students take notes after they have read long paragraphs in the section rather than the entire chapter. This helps them focus on important ideas and details and prevents them from losing track of the flow of information. Remind students that as they take notes on the section, they should not take a long time to do it. Students should read, think, write, and move on.

Chapter 5 **FOLDABLES**

China and Its Neighbors

CHAPTER SUMMARY

China has very diverse landforms, and its civilization is more than 4,000 years old. Its communist leaders have changed the economy to give the people more economic freedom, and the economy has grown rapidly as a result. The ancient teachings of Kongfuzi, Daoism, and Buddhism still influence the people of China. Taiwan is an island off the southeast coast of China and is a bustling center of trade and commerce. Mongolia, located between China and Russia, used to be a land of nomads, but today about 60 percent of Mongols live in urban areas.

CHAPTER PREVIEW

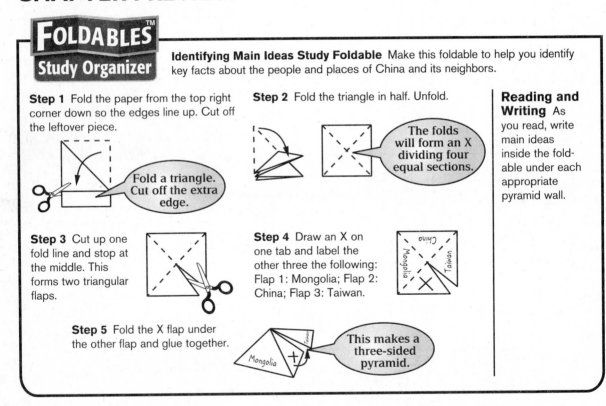

FOLDABLES™ Study Organizer

Identifying Main Ideas Study Foldable Make this foldable to help you identify key facts about the people and places of China and its neighbors.

Step 1 Fold the paper from the top right corner down so the edges line up. Cut off the leftover piece.

Fold a triangle. Cut off the extra edge.

Step 2 Fold the triangle in half. Unfold.

The folds will form an X dividing four equal sections.

Reading and Writing As you read, write main ideas inside the fold-able under each appropriate pyramid wall.

Step 3 Cut up one fold line and stop at the middle. This forms two triangular flaps.

Step 4 Draw an X on one tab and label the other three the following: Flap 1: Mongolia; Flap 2: China; Flap 3: Taiwan.

Step 5 Fold the X flap under the other flap and glue together.

This makes a three-sided pyramid.

CHAPTER REVIEW

Foldables Follow-Up Activity

Organize students into pairs. Have one student point to a country on their foldable's pyramid wall. The other student should say the main ideas aloud that he or she remembers as his or her partner checks the ideas off on the foldable using a pencil. Each identified main idea counts for two points. Students should switch roles, and be sure to list the main ideas about all countries. The student with the most points wins the game.

Alternative Activities for Chapter 6

IDENTIFYING

Have students make a pyramid foldable for pictures representative of China. Suggest they find books, newspaper articles, or magazine articles about China. Have students gather information, photocopy several pictures, and then sketch three things they think capture the essence of China the most. Encourage students to use colored pencils and to share their final products with other students.

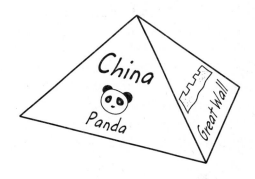

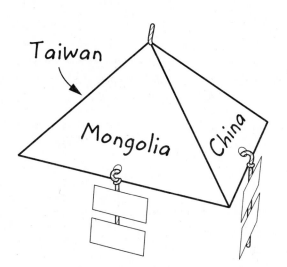

DESCRIBING

Have students cut off the tip of their foldables, run a piece of yarn through them, and tie a knot. Then students should punch holes on each side of the pyramid and thread yarn through them. Students should then make information cards about China and its neighbors. Cards might contain interesting facts or map sketches. Tape the cards to the yarn and hang the mobiles throughout the classroom.

Student Study Tip

There are several review tools that students can use in order to prepare for tests. Students can create study checklists to identify the material they are responsible for and organize the material into manageable chunks. They can outline the chapter and then quiz themselves on the main ideas of the outline. Students can also create flashcards for vocabulary terms.

Chapter 6 FOLDABLES

Japan and the Koreas

CHAPTER SUMMARY

Japan has few mineral resources, but its people have built a strong industrial economy through trade, the use of advanced technology, and a highly skilled workforce. Japan is a group of islands located in the western Pacific Ocean. Its land is mountainous but with intensive cultivation, its limited farmland is productive. The Japanese people have been strongly influenced by China and by Western countries. South Korea and North Korea share the same peninsula and history, but they have different political and economic systems. After World War II, the peninsula was divided into two countries, with a communist government in North Korea and a non-communist government in South Korea.

CHAPTER PREVIEW

Compare-Contrast Study Foldable Make this foldable to help you compare and contrast the people and places of Japan and the Koreas.

Step 1 Fold one sheet of paper in half from top to bottom.

Step 2 Fold it in half again, from side to side.

Reading and Writing As you read the chapter, write what you learn about these countries under the appropriate tab. Use your notes to determine how these countries are alike and different.

Step 3 Unfold the paper once. Sketch an outline of the Koreas and Japan across both tabs and label them as shown.

Step 4 Cut up the fold of the top flap only.

This cut will make two tabs.

CHAPTER REVIEW

Foldables Follow-Up Activity

Once students have completed their foldables, have them locate the countries on a map. Ask them to think about how these countries are different from their own, and to write a letter to a potential pen pal in one of the countries. Encourage them to share what they think they have in common in their letters, and to ask questions about the other person's country. Have volunteers read their letters to the class.

Alternative Activities for Chapter 7

COMPARE AND CONTRAST

Using the same foldable design, ask students to compare and contrast North Korea and South Korea. Students should write what they have learned about these two countries under the appropriate tab. Encourage students to do research outside of class to find the most recent information about North and South Korea. Make sure students' research is thorough.

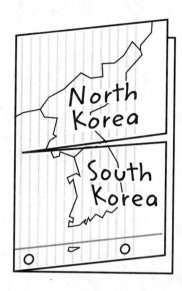

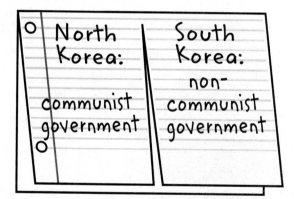

ANALYZING

Have students compare and contrast the communist government in North Korea and the non-communist government in South Korea. Students should list their findings under the appropriate tab with information from their textbooks. Then organize students into small groups to identify the pros and cons of each form of government.

Student Study Tip

Remind students that it is important to think before writing an essay. Brainstorming in groups can be especially helpful to produce ideas or topics. Make sure students understand what is being asked of them and to ask questions if they are confused. If students are not under a time constraint, encourage them to write several drafts before writing the final essay.

Chapter 7 FOLDABLES

Southeast Asia

CHAPTER SUMMARY

Southeast Asia consists of mainland and island countries. Agriculture is a major source of income in the countries of mainland Southeast Asia. As a result of war, Laos, Cambodia, and Vietnam are the most economically disadvantaged countries of mainland Southeast Asia. The island countries of Southeast Asia include Indonesia, Malaysia, Singapore, Brunei, and the Philippines. Indonesia is the largest country in Southeast Asia and the fourth most-populous country in the world. Indonesia's leaders face the challenge of creating a nation out of a land with many different groups and political parties.

CHAPTER PREVIEW

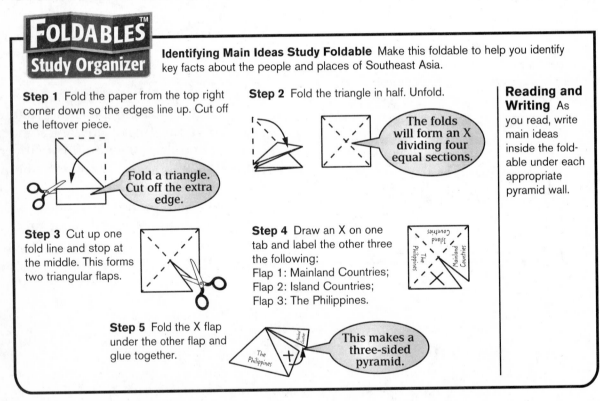

FOLDABLES™
Study Organizer

Identifying Main Ideas Study Foldable Make this foldable to help you identify key facts about the people and places of Southeast Asia.

Step 1 Fold the paper from the top right corner down so the edges line up. Cut off the leftover piece.

Fold a triangle. Cut off the extra edge.

Step 2 Fold the triangle in half. Unfold.

The folds will form an X dividing four equal sections.

Step 3 Cut up one fold line and stop at the middle. This forms two triangular flaps.

Step 4 Draw an X on one tab and label the other three the following:
Flap 1: Mainland Countries;
Flap 2: Island Countries;
Flap 3: The Philippines.

Step 5 Fold the X flap under the other flap and glue together.

This makes a three-sided pyramid.

Reading and Writing As you read, write main ideas inside the foldable under each appropriate pyramid wall.

CHAPTER REVIEW

Foldables Follow-Up Activity

Organize students into small groups to create a map of Southeast Asia. On a poster board, students should draw the region of Southeast Asia, label each country, and use different colored markers or pencils to illustrate political boundaries. Have students use their foldables to write captions that reflect the main ideas about the countries of Southeast Asia. Display the maps around the classroom.

Alternative Activities for Chapter 8

IDENTIFYING

Have students create this pyramid foldable to identify basic facts about the economy, people, and geography of a country in Southeast Asia. Students may want to use newspaper articles or the Internet to find additional information about the country. When students have completed their foldables, have them share the information they found with the class.

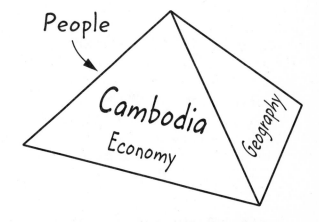

PREDICTING CONSEQUENCES

Have students use this pyramid foldable to identify facts about the past and present conditions of a country in Southeast Asia. Students should describe how conflicts, natural disasters, or political groups have affected, and still influence, the country's people and economy. On the third side of the pyramid, have students predict how economic or political events might impact the country in the future. Have students share their predictions with the class.

Student Study Tip

Remind students that certain words or phrases can be clues to help them understand what type of information is being presented. Words such as *first*, *next*, or *last* show chronological order, whereas phrases such as *that is why* or *as a result* demonstrate cause-and-effect relationships. Students should be aware of these clues as they read about a country's economic and political development.

Chapter 8 FOLDABLES

Europe–Early History

CHAPTER SUMMARY

Ancient Greece and Rome made important contributions to Western culture and civilization. The beginnings of the West's political system can be traced to Athens, Greece, where the first democratic constitution was written. In the Roman Republic, consuls were elected by the people and served in the Roman Senate. Senators, however, lost power to emperors when the Roman Republic became the Roman Empire. The Roman Empire declined when Germanic peoples invaded. The Catholic Church soon became the major political power in western Europe. During the Renaissance, the study of science, art, and education was renewed, and nations were created, uniting people with common languages and cultures.

CHAPTER PREVIEW

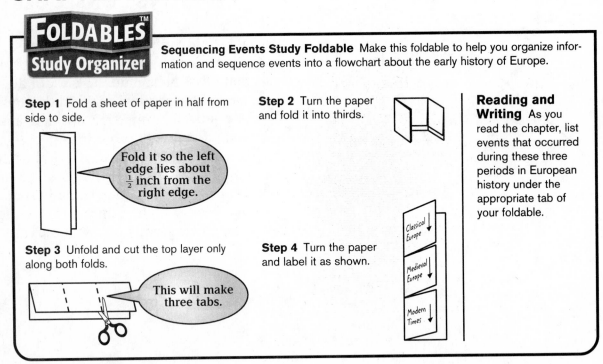

FOLDABLES™ **Study Organizer**

Sequencing Events Study Foldable Make this foldable to help you organize information and sequence events into a flowchart about the early history of Europe.

Step 1 Fold a sheet of paper in half from side to side.

Fold it so the left edge lies about $\frac{1}{2}$ inch from the right edge.

Step 2 Turn the paper and fold it into thirds.

Reading and Writing As you read the chapter, list events that occurred during these three periods in European history under the appropriate tab of your foldable.

Step 3 Unfold and cut the top layer only along both folds.

This will make three tabs.

Step 4 Turn the paper and label it as shown.

Classical Europe

Medieval Europe

Modern Times

CHAPTER REVIEW

Foldables Follow-Up Activity

Have students work in pairs to quiz each other using their foldables. One student should describe an event that occurred in western Europe during classical, medieval, or modern times. The other student should identify in which time period the event occurred. Have students keep score, and the student who identifies the correct period the most number of times wins.

Alternative Activities for Chapter 9

ORGANIZING

To help students organize information about Greece, the Roman Republic, and the Roman Empire, have students create a foldable like the one shown. Students should take notes that describe the main ideas about each time period and write them under the appropriate tab. Have students share their notes with a partner and adjust their foldables to account for any main ideas that they did not identify.

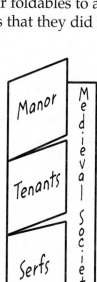

DESCRIBING

Have students create this foldable to describe the elements of the feudal estate. Under each appropriate tab, students should define manor, tenants, and serfs, and list any additional information that will help them remember the definitions. Encourage students to draw a web diagram to better understand how feudalism worked.

Student Study Tip

To help students take notes on the information presented in their textbooks, have them convert each main head in the section into a question. Students should use words such as *who, what, where, when,* or *why* to form their questions. For example, students might ask: What was the Golden Age of Greece? After students have created their questions, they should read the section to find the answers.

Chapter 9 **FOLDABLES**

Europe–Modern History

CHAPTER SUMMARY

Europe has played a major role in shaping today's world. Competition for markets and resources as a result of industrialization led to imperialism and friction among European countries during the 1800s. The democratic United States and the Communist Soviet Union competed to bring their forms of government to the nations of post-World War II Europe, causing a cold war. At the end of the Cold War, old and new nations of Europe faced many challenges. The fall of the Soviet Union in the early 1990s increased Europe's global influence and strengthened the movement towards greater political and economic unity. Problems still remain in Europe, however, including poverty, population growth, and pollution.

CHAPTER PREVIEW

FOLDABLES™
Study Organizer

Summarizing Information Study Foldable Make the following foldable to help you organize and summarize information about historic events and modern events in Europe, and how they are related.

Step 1 Fold a sheet of paper from side to side, leaving a 2-inch tab uncovered along the side.

Fold it so the left edge lies 2 inches from the right edge.

Step 2 Turn the paper and fold it into thirds.

Step 3 Unfold and cut along the two inside fold lines.

Cut along the two folds on the front flap to make 3 tabs.

Step 4 Label the foldable as shown.

EUROPE: MODERN HISTORY
The Modern Era | Continent Divided | Move Toward Unity

Reading and Writing As you read about the modern history of Europe, write important facts under each appropriate tab of your foldable.

CHAPTER REVIEW

Foldables Follow-Up Activity

Have students use their foldables to create a time line of events of Europe in the modern era. Organize students into groups of four and have them use the events listed on their foldables to create a time line on poster board. Time line ranges should include the years from 1700 to 2002. Students should choose events from their foldables that they feel were significant in the development of a unified Europe. Students may want to illustrate specific events or people who played a major role in Europe from the eighteenth century to the present.

Alternative Activities for Chapter 10

ORGANIZING

Have students create a foldable to help them remember information about Europe during the first half of the twentieth century. Students should label their tabs *World War I*, *Between the World Wars*, and *World War II*. Have them research the chapter and other sources for facts and main ideas and write the information under the correct tab. Remind them to use their foldables as they study for quizzes and tests.

EVALUATING

Have students create a foldable that addresses the challenges Europe faces today. Students should use the Internet to find information about poverty, population growth, and pollution in Europe. Have students write facts about the issues and how European countries are trying to address them on their foldables. Ask students to evaluate whether they think European nations are taking the necessary steps to resolve the issues.

Student Study Tip

Remind students that they should preview the information in a chapter before they read. Students should read the chapter title and try to formulate an idea of what they will be learning. They should then read the subtitles within each section to see how the main idea is developed. Have students skim the photos, charts, graphs, or maps, and ask them to think about how they support the main idea.

Chapter 10 FOLDABLES

CHAPTER II

Western Europe Today

CHAPTER SUMMARY

Although they are members of the European Union, western European countries are economically and politically diverse. Western European countries are generally industrialized, with much of the countries' populations working in the manufacturing and service industries. Agriculture, however, is also an important industry for countries such as the Netherlands and Greece. As the economies vary throughout the countries of western Europe, so do the different types of governments. Governments include republics and constitutional monarchies. Although different, western European countries have united to form the European Union, making the region an even stronger economic and political world power.

CHAPTER PREVIEW

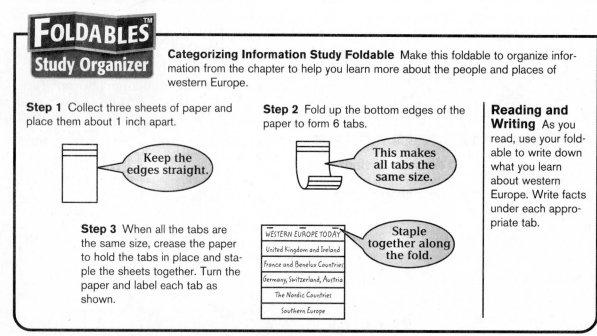

FOLDABLES™
Study Organizer

Categorizing Information Study Foldable Make this foldable to organize information from the chapter to help you learn more about the people and places of western Europe.

Step 1 Collect three sheets of paper and place them about 1 inch apart.

Keep the edges straight.

Step 2 Fold up the bottom edges of the paper to form 6 tabs.

This makes all tabs the same size.

Step 3 When all the tabs are the same size, crease the paper to hold the tabs in place and staple the sheets together. Turn the paper and label each tab as shown.

WESTERN EUROPE TODAY
United Kingdom and Ireland
France and Benelux Countries
Germany, Switzerland, Austria
The Nordic Countries
Southern Europe

Staple together along the fold.

Reading and Writing As you read, use your foldable to write down what you learn about western Europe. Write facts under each appropriate tab.

CHAPTER REVIEW

Foldables Follow-Up Activity

Once students have created their foldables about western Europe, organize them into small groups. Then have the groups design museum exhibits that show the history and modern times of one or several of the countries in western Europe. They may have to do outside research for more historical information. They should sketch out the plan and write a description of the exhibit. Ask them to share their ideas with the rest of the class.

Alternative Activities for Chapter 11

DESCRIBING

Have students create foldables that contain interesting facts about Belgium, the Netherlands, and Luxembourg. Students might want to use the Internet to find additional information about the Benelux countries' economies, government, and people. When completed, have students create a travel brochure with illustrations that highlights these facts. Have volunteers share their brochures with the class.

```
THE BENELUX COUNTRIES
Belgium
The Netherlands
Luxembourg
```

```
FRANCE
geography
people
economy
```

COMPARING

Have students choose a country from western Europe and use the Internet to research its geography, people, and economy. Students should write the information on their foldables under the appropriate tab. Ask students to share the information they found with the class and compare the countries they researched. Have students choose a country they would like to visit and explain why.

Student Study Tip

Before students read about each country in western Europe, refer them to the physical map of Europe on pages RA18–RA19 in their textbooks. Students should locate the country on the map and identify its capital. Have students study the map and speculate how physical features such as rivers, seas, and mountains might influence the country's people and economy.

Chapter 11 FOLDABLES

Eastern Europe Today

CHAPTER SUMMARY

The fall of communism has greatly affected the economies of eastern Europe, both positively and negatively. Closer economic ties to western Europe have helped some countries move toward free-market economies. Mining and manufacturing are important economic activities for countries such as Poland, whereas tourism and high-technology manufacturing are vital for the Czech Republic. Some countries, however, have suffered from ethnic conflicts and economic setbacks that have prevented them from experiencing economic development. Ethnic conflicts have torn apart the former Yugoslav Republics, and lack of money has prevented Albania from mining its country's rich minerals. The struggle to achieve economic prosperity continues for the people of the former Soviet republics.

CHAPTER PREVIEW

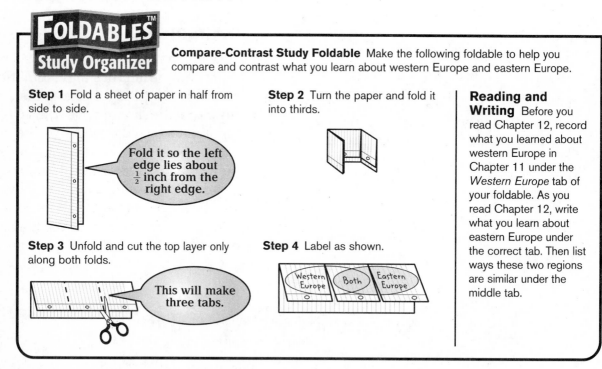

FOLDABLES™
Study Organizer

Compare-Contrast Study Foldable Make the following foldable to help you compare and contrast what you learn about western Europe and eastern Europe.

Step 1 Fold a sheet of paper in half from side to side.

Fold it so the left edge lies about $\frac{1}{2}$ inch from the right edge.

Step 2 Turn the paper and fold it into thirds.

Step 3 Unfold and cut the top layer only along both folds.

This will make three tabs.

Step 4 Label as shown.

Western Europe   Both   Eastern Europe

Reading and Writing Before you read Chapter 12, record what you learned about western Europe in Chapter 11 under the *Western Europe* tab of your foldable. As you read Chapter 12, write what you learn about eastern Europe under the correct tab. Then list ways these two regions are similar under the middle tab.

CHAPTER REVIEW

Foldables Follow-Up Activity

Have students use their foldables to write a paragraph explaining the similarities and differences between western Europe and eastern Europe. Students should explain how these differences have benefited or harmed different countries within the region. Have volunteers share their paragraphs with the class and ask students if they agree or disagree with their classmates' conclusions and explain why.

Alternative Activities for Chapter 12

EXPLAINING

Have students choose a country in eastern Europe to research. Students should use the Internet or magazines to find information about the similarities and differences between the country's history and its situation today and write this information on their foldables. Students should focus on how political and social events have positively or negatively impacted the country. Have students explain the information they found to the class.

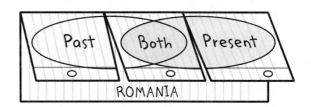

COMPARE AND CONTRAST

Students should create foldables that highlight the differences and similarities between rural and urban life in eastern Europe today. Students should use the Internet to research what life is like in eastern Europe for rural and urban populations and record the information on their foldables. As a class, discuss life in rural and urban areas in the United States. Ask students to describe the similarities and differences between the two regions.

Student Study Tip

If a word's meaning is unknown, have students reread the sentences that precede or follow it to see if its meaning can be derived from the context. If students have difficulty using deciphering and context clues to figure out a word's meaning, have them find the word in the Glossary or a dictionary. Students should write the definition in their notes so they do not have to look it up again.

Chapter 12 FOLDABLES

Russia and Its Neighbors

CHAPTER SUMMARY

Russia is the largest country in the world. It expands from Europe to Asia and has diverse geographic features such as the Ural and Caucasus Mountains and the western plains. Because of its vast size, rivers and railroads are vital for moving goods throughout Russia. To the south are the Eurasian Republics where many different ethnic groups live. The Caucasus Republics have struggled to develop their own industries and businesses since the collapse of the Soviet Union and are facing many ethnic conflicts. The population of Russia consists of more than 150 different ethnic groups who have contributed to Russia's rich tradition of art, music, and literature.

CHAPTER PREVIEW

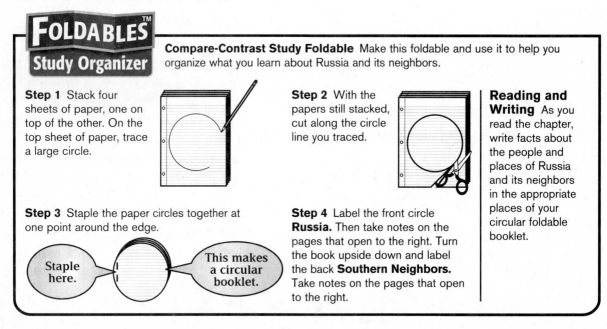

FOLDABLES™
Study Organizer

Compare-Contrast Study Foldable Make this foldable and use it to help you organize what you learn about Russia and its neighbors.

Step 1 Stack four sheets of paper, one on top of the other. On the top sheet of paper, trace a large circle.

Step 2 With the papers still stacked, cut along the circle line you traced.

Reading and Writing As you read the chapter, write facts about the people and places of Russia and its neighbors in the appropriate places of your circular foldable booklet.

Step 3 Staple the paper circles together at one point around the edge.

Staple here.

This makes a circular booklet.

Step 4 Label the front circle **Russia.** Then take notes on the pages that open to the right. Turn the book upside down and label the back **Southern Neighbors.** Take notes on the pages that open to the right.

CHAPTER REVIEW

Foldables Follow-Up Activity

Organize students into pairs and have each pair write three sentences that summarize the main ideas of Chapter 13. Students' sentences should address Russia's geography and descriptions of its population. Have students share the sentences that they wrote with the class and ask them to vote for the one that they think best summarizes the chapter.

Alternative Activities for Chapter 13

IDENTIFYING

Have students create circular foldable booklets about two geographic features in Russia. For example, students might research the Ural Mountains and the Volga River. Students should find information about the physical features and why they are important to Russia. The first feature should be written on the front of the booklet and students should write facts inside. Then have students turn the book upside down and write facts for the second feature on the opposite pages.

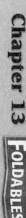

COMPARE AND CONTRAST

Have students create a foldable that compares and contrasts the lifestyles of people from two of the Eurasian Republics. Students should use the Internet and their textbooks for information about physical features, climate, economic activity, and ethnic groups. Students may illustrate this information in the form of graphs and charts.

Student Study Tip

Information from the Internet is useful to students, but it should be reviewed critically. As students read information sources, remind them to think about the author's biases. Students should try to identify the author's purpose for writing the information and how the author sometimes tries to influence the reader's opinion of the subject material.

Chapter 13

FOLDABLES

Russia–Past and Present

CHAPTER SUMMARY

Emperors called czars ruled the Russian Empire from 1480 to 1917. Russians blamed the czar for food shortages and the casualties brought about by World War I. The czar was overthrown in 1917 and a communist state was established. In 1922 the Union of Soviet Socialist Republics, or the Soviet Union, was formed and included Russia and most of the conquered territories of the old Russian Empire. Through industrialization and military buildup, the Soviet Union became a world power. After World War II, the United States and the Soviet Union engaged in a cold war, competing for world influence without actually fighting. In 1991 the Soviet Union broke apart, and Russia became an independent republic. Russia faces challenges in adopting a free market economy and a democratic government.

CHAPTER PREVIEW

Categorizing Information Study Foldable When you group information into categories, it is easier to make sense of what you are learning. Make this foldable to help you learn about Russia's past and present.

Step 1 Fold one sheet of paper in half from top to bottom.

Step 2 Fold it in half again, from side to side.

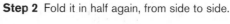

Step 3 Unfold the paper once. Cut up the inside fold of the top flap only.

This cut will make two tabs.

Step 4 Turn the paper and sketch a map of the USSR and Russia on the front tabs. Label your foldable as shown.

Past
USSR
Present
Russia

Reading and Writing As you read the chapter, write under the appropriate flaps of your foldable what you learn about the former USSR and present-day Russia.

CHAPTER REVIEW

Foldables Follow-Up Activity

Have students work in small groups to quiz each other about the differences between the former USSR and present-day Russia. Have students read a characteristic or feature that they noted on their foldables. The other students should decide whether that description refers to either the USSR or Russia. Have students edit their foldables to account for any information that they did not list.

Alternative Activities for Chapter 14

DESCRIBING

Have students use the Internet to find information about "Ivan the Great" and "Ivan the Terrible" and write it on their foldables under the appropriate tab. Write *Accomplishments* on the board. Have students use their foldables to describe the accomplishments of the first czars as you note them on the board. Ask students to explain how these first czars served as models for czars who ruled after them.

EXPLAINING

Students should use the Internet and magazines to find facts about what life was like in communist Russia and what life is like today for Russians under the free enterprise system. Students should write these descriptions under the appropriate tabs on their foldables. When they have completed their foldables, organize the class into two groups to debate which economic system works best for Russia.

Student Study Tip

Before students answer the question about a map, chart, or graph, remind them to study the graphic carefully to understand what information is being presented and what is being asked in the question. Students should read the title, labels, keys, or axes to learn about the graphic's subject and note how the data is organized.

Chapter 14 **FOLDABLES**

East and Central Africa

CHAPTER SUMMARY

Both Kenya and Tanzania are countries of diverse landscapes and peoples. The western part of Kenya is marked by highlands and the wide Great Rift Valley. Coffee and tea are grown for export, and tourism is a major industry. Farming and tourism are the main economic activities in Tanzania. The other countries of East Africa have all been scarred by conflict in recent years. For example, Sudan has been torn by a civil war between the northern Muslim Arabs and the southern Christian peoples. Central Africa has rich natural resources that are largely undeveloped because of civil war and poor government decisions. Although the Democratic Republic of the Congo has many resources, it has not been able to take advantage of them because of a recent civil war.

CHAPTER PREVIEW

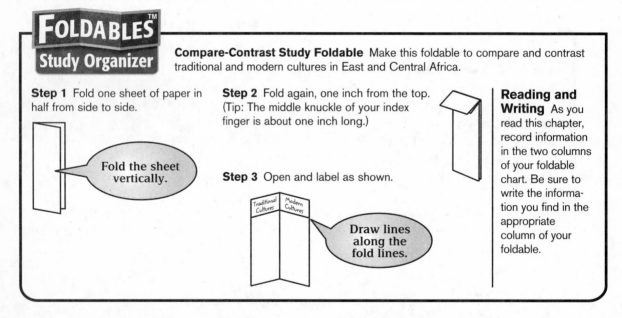

FOLDABLES™
Study Organizer

Compare-Contrast Study Foldable Make this foldable to compare and contrast traditional and modern cultures in East and Central Africa.

Step 1 Fold one sheet of paper in half from side to side.

Fold the sheet vertically.

Step 2 Fold again, one inch from the top. (Tip: The middle knuckle of your index finger is about one inch long.)

Step 3 Open and label as shown.

Traditional Cultures | Modern Cultures

Draw lines along the fold lines.

Reading and Writing As you read this chapter, record information in the two columns of your foldable chart. Be sure to write the information you find in the appropriate column of your foldable.

CHAPTER REVIEW

Foldables Follow-Up Activity

Organize the class into two groups. One group of students will represent the traditional cultures of East and Central Africa. The other group will represent the modern cultures of East and Central Africa. Individual members of each group will take turns reciting one fact that they have written on their foldables. Each group member of both groups should be able to recite one fact. Then ask student volunteers to briefly answer this question: How are traditional and modern cultures similar in East and Central Africa?

Alternative Activities for Chapter 15

IDENTIFYING

Have students choose to examine either East Africa or Central Africa. Then have them create this foldable and label it according to their choice. Students should complete their foldables by focusing first on the past histories, governments, and economies of the countries within East Africa (or Central Africa). Then students should describe the current situations/events and economies in those same countries. By doing this, students will have created a brief history of the countries in East or Central Africa.

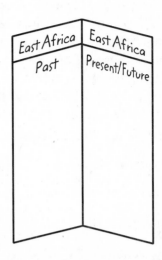

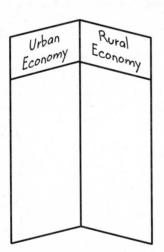

COMPARING

As students read the chapter, have them take notes that compare the urban and rural economies of East and Central Africa. Students should describe each type of economy as they operate in different parts of East and Central Africa. Students should also be able to name the countries of East and Central Africa and the types of economies they possess.

Student Study Tip

Tell students that one good way to complete reading assignments is to first read the entire section. Although students should take their time and pause and reread when needed to understand the material, they should not stop to take notes yet. After the first reading, they should review the material again and then take notes on the important concepts, people, and places.

Chapter 15 FOLDABLES

West Africa

CHAPTER SUMMARY

Nigeria is a large, oil-rich country in West Africa. It has more people than any other African nation. Nigeria's major landforms are coastal lowlands, savannas, highlands, plateaus, and partly dry grasslands. More than 90 percent of Nigeria's income comes from oil exports. The country has more than 300 ethnic groups. The four largest groups are the Hausa, Fulani, Yoruba, and Ibo. Other countries of West Africa, known as the Sahel countries, face a continuing struggle to keep grasslands from turning into desert, but the coastal countries receive plenty of rainfall. The Sahel countries are Mauritania, Mali, Niger, Chad, and Burkina Faso. The 11 countries that make up coastal West Africa are Senegal, Gambia, Guinea, Guinea-Bissau, Cape Verde, Liberia, Sierra Leone, Côte d'Ivoire, Ghana, Togo, and Benin.

CHAPTER PREVIEW

Summarizing Information Study Foldable Make this foldable to determine what you already know, to identify what you want to know, and to summarize what you learn about West Africa.

Step 1 Fold a sheet of paper into thirds from top to bottom.

Step 2 Turn the paper horizontally, unfold, and label the three columns as shown.

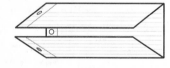

Reading and Writing
Before you read the chapter, write what you already know about West Africa under the "Know" tab. Write what you want to know about West Africa under the "Want to Know" tab. Then, as you read the chapter, write what you learn under the "Learned" tab. Be sure to include information you wanted to know (from the second column).

CHAPTER REVIEW

Foldables Follow-Up Activity

After all members of the class have completed their foldable activities, ask: Did you learn what you wanted to learn? Call on student volunteers to recite the information that they wanted to know before creating the foldable and what they learned after they read the chapter. Then ask students to write an answer to this question: What would you like to learn more about in West Africa? Have students work individually or in groups to complete some additional research on West Africa.

Alternative Activities for Chapter 16

SUMMARIZING

Have students create and complete this foldable by describing each of three great African empires that existed from the A.D. 500s to the 1500s. Students should write as much information under each column heading as they can find. You may want to encourage students to do additional research either individually or in groups to complete the foldable.

Ancient African Empires		
Ghana	Mali	Songhai

Hausa	Fulani	Yoruba	Ibo

ANALYZING

To complete this foldable, students will need to fold a sheet of paper into fourths in Step 1. (They must fold a sheet of paper in half, then in half again.) Then students should turn the paper horizontally and label the four columns as shown. Students should then research these four ethnic groups of Nigeria at the library and write as much information as they can under each column heading. Have students compare the information they found after they have completed their foldables.

Student Study Tip

Encourage students to spend some time becoming familiar with using library resources. Students should explore these various types of reference books: encyclopedias, biographical dictionaries, atlases, and almanacs. Students may use card catalogs, periodical guides, and/or computer databases to help them find the information they need.

Chapter 16 FOLDABLES

South Africa and Its Neighbors

CHAPTER SUMMARY

South Africa has recently seen major social and political changes. In 1994 South Africa held its first democratic election in which people from all ethnic groups could vote. Because of its abundant mineral resources, it has the most industrialized economy in Africa. The inland countries of southern Africa are landlocked and experience a mild climate. Most of the people practice subsistence farming, and thousands move to cities each year to find work. Southern Africa's Atlantic and Indian Ocean countries are struggling to develop their economies.

CHAPTER PREVIEW

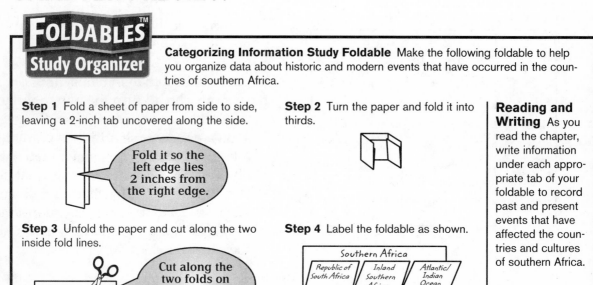

FOLDABLES™
Study Organizer

Categorizing Information Study Foldable Make the following foldable to help you organize data about historic and modern events that have occurred in the countries of southern Africa.

Step 1 Fold a sheet of paper from side to side, leaving a 2-inch tab uncovered along the side.

Fold it so the left edge lies 2 inches from the right edge.

Step 2 Turn the paper and fold it into thirds.

Step 3 Unfold the paper and cut along the two inside fold lines.

Cut along the two folds on the front flap to make 3 tabs.

Step 4 Label the foldable as shown.

Southern Africa

Republic of South Africa | Inland Southern Africa | Atlantic/ Indian Ocean Countries

Reading and Writing As you read the chapter, write information under each appropriate tab of your foldable to record past and present events that have affected the countries and cultures of southern Africa.

CHAPTER REVIEW

Foldables Follow-Up Activity

Have students work in small groups and choose a past or present event described in their foldables that has affected one of the countries of southern Africa. Students should research the event using newspapers and the Internet and then perform a short skit about it. As a class, discuss each skit and whether or not the skit appeared factually accurate. Have the class vote for the best skit.

Alternative Activities for Chapter 17

PREDICTING

Have students research major events that have occurred in South Africa's history and write them under the appropriate foldable tab. They should then review newspapers and magazines for articles about current events in South Africa and write these under the second tab. Using the information that they found, students should look for any cause-and-effect relationships. Ask students to speculate how these events might influence the future of South Africa and write their predictions under the third tab. Have students share their predictions with the class and explain how they were derived.

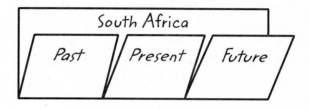

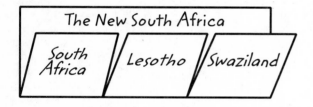

CATEGORIZING

Have students research information using their textbooks and the Internet about the economies of South Africa, Lesotho, and Swaziland and write the information under the appropriate tab. Students should write an essay that summarizes the challenges that Lesotho and Swaziland face as enclaves and describe what actions they might take to become more independent of South Africa.

Student Study Tip

Help students understand vocabulary terms by looking for common prefixes and suffixes. Common prefixes include *anti-*: "opposed to"; *com/con*: "together"; and *non/un*: "not." Common suffixes include *ation*: "process of"; *ism*: "practice"; and *ology*: "the study of."

Chapter 17 FOLDABLES

Canada

CHAPTER SUMMARY

Canada is the second-largest country in the world and has many landforms, climates, resources, and people. Canada's economy is rich in fertile farmland, natural resources, and skilled workers. Canada's government is a parliamentary democracy headed by a prime minister. Quebec and Ontario are the largest provinces in Canada and contain the most people. Canadians of many different backgrounds live in towns and cities located near the United States border. Inuit and Native Americans were the first Canadians. Then French and British settlers built homes there. Recently, large numbers of immigrants have arrived from Asia and eastern Europe.

CHAPTER PREVIEW

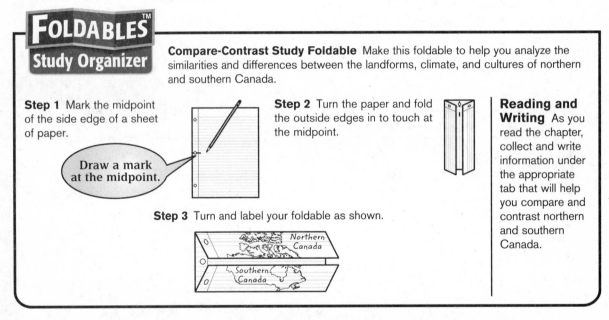

FOLDABLES™ Study Organizer

Compare-Contrast Study Foldable Make this foldable to help you analyze the similarities and differences between the landforms, climate, and cultures of northern and southern Canada.

Step 1 Mark the midpoint of the side edge of a sheet of paper.

Draw a mark at the midpoint.

Step 2 Turn the paper and fold the outside edges in to touch at the midpoint.

Reading and Writing As you read the chapter, collect and write information under the appropriate tab that will help you compare and contrast northern and southern Canada.

Step 3 Turn and label your foldable as shown.

Northern Canada

Southern Canada

CHAPTER REVIEW

Foldables Follow-Up Activity

Have students work in small groups to play a guessing game using their completed foldables. Have each student in the group take turns choosing a fact from his or her completed foldable and recite it to the rest of the group. Group members will guess whether the recited fact describes northern Canada or southern Canada. The student that guesses the region correctly is the next to recite a fact from his or her foldable. Have students continue the game until every student has had an opportunity to recite a fact.

Alternative Activities for Chapter 18

SUMMARIZING

Have students create and use this foldable to review Canada's provinces and territories. Students should list the 10 provinces and the three territories under each appropriate tab. Students should also include at least one fact that describes each province and territory on their foldables.

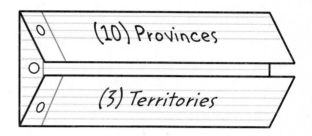

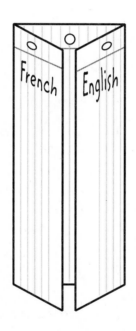

DESCRIBING

Students should create the foldable as shown and then turn it so that the outside edges open outward. On the left foldable tab students should write *French* and on the right tab, they should write *English.* Students are then ready to take notes about Canada's bilingual history under each appropriate tab. As a follow-up activity, have students research to find out more about Canada's bilingual history and write the information in the center of the foldable.

Student Study Tip

As students are learning about Canada, have them create a question bank for each section. Students should change each subhead into a question. For example, the first head in Section 1 is "Landforms and Climate." Students might ask, "What landforms and climate are found in Canada?" Students should provide an answer for each question. They may then use their question bank to prepare for the chapter test.

Chapter 18 **FOLDABLES**

The United States

CHAPTER SUMMARY

The United States is a country with a great variety of landforms and climates. It has five main physical regions: the Coastal Plains, the Appalachian Mountains, the Interior Plains, the Mountains and Plateaus region, and the Pacific Coast. Alaska and Hawaii make up two more regions. The United States economy thrives as a result of abundant resources and the hard work of Americans. It has emerged as the world's most productive economy. Immigrants from all over the world have come to the United States, creating a land of many cultures. The United States has a representative democratic government with power shared by the states and the national government.

CHAPTER PREVIEW

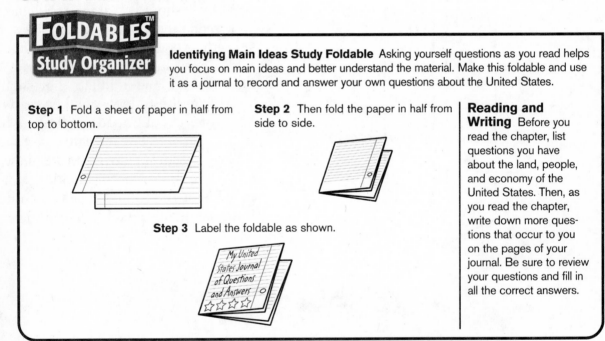

Identifying Main Ideas Study Foldable Asking yourself questions as you read helps you focus on main ideas and better understand the material. Make this foldable and use it as a journal to record and answer your own questions about the United States.

Step 1 Fold a sheet of paper in half from top to bottom.

Step 2 Then fold the paper in half from side to side.

Reading and Writing Before you read the chapter, list questions you have about the land, people, and economy of the United States. Then, as you read the chapter, write down more questions that occur to you on the pages of your journal. Be sure to review your questions and fill in all the correct answers.

Step 3 Label the foldable as shown.

My United States Journal of Questions and Answers

CHAPTER REVIEW

Foldables Follow-Up Activity

Organize students into pairs to discuss the questions they wrote in their foldables. Then have the students try to answer each other's questions. As students engage in their discussions, monitor their progress, stopping to ask groups questions of your own about the chapter. You may want to award bonus points for correct answers.

Alternative Activities for Chapter 19

DESCRIBING

Have students create foldables to describe the physical regions of the United States. Students should label their foldables as shown, and then describe each of the physical regions of the country on the inside of their foldables. Students may then use their completed foldables as study guides for Section 1 of this chapter.

ORGANIZING

Have students create a foldable as shown to organize information about the different ethnic groups living in the United States. Students should include the following groups in their foldables: Europeans, African Americans, Hispanics, Asian Americans, Pacific Islanders, and Native Americans. Students should then write facts about each group under the appropriate heading. Encourage students to do additional research to complete their foldables.

Student Study Tip

Advise students to prepare for chapter essay tests not only by reviewing their notes, but also by carefully identifying the major content areas of the chapter that they need to learn. For example, they might want to create a list of possible topics for essay questions, and then study those topics. Students should examine their lists and reread or examine topics that they do not completely understand.

Chapter 19 FOLDABLES

Mexico

CHAPTER SUMMARY

Mexico's mountainous landscape and varied climate have led to the creation of three different economic regions. Northern Mexico is known for producing steel and cement. Central Mexico is the country's heartland and most of the people live in this region for its pleasant weather, industrial opportunities, and fertile soil. Subsistence farms and plantations inhabit most of southern Mexico—the country's poorest region. Mexico's culture reflects a combination of Native American and Spanish influences. Mexico won its independence from Spain in 1821, and today Mexico is a federal republic. Mexico is plagued by problems caused by population growth, foreign investment and debt, and pollution.

CHAPTER PREVIEW

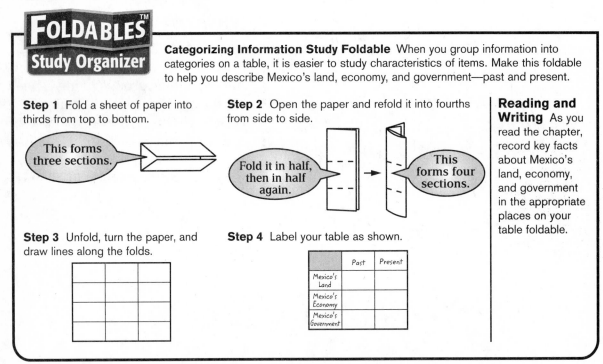

Categorizing Information Study Foldable When you group information into categories on a table, it is easier to study characteristics of items. Make this foldable to help you describe Mexico's land, economy, and government—past and present.

Step 1 Fold a sheet of paper into thirds from top to bottom.

This forms three sections.

Step 2 Open the paper and refold it into fourths from side to side.

Fold it in half, then in half again.

This forms four sections.

Step 3 Unfold, turn the paper, and draw lines along the folds.

Step 4 Label your table as shown.

	Past	Present
Mexico's Land		
Mexico's Economy		
Mexico's Government		

Reading and Writing As you read the chapter, record key facts about Mexico's land, economy, and government in the appropriate places on your table foldable.

CHAPTER REVIEW

Foldables Follow-Up Activity

After students have completed their foldables, they should be able to compare and contrast past and present facts about Mexico's land, economy, and government. Have each student select one area on which to focus (or assign students one of the three areas). Have students write a brief essay that compares the past and present of Mexico's land, economy, or government.

Alternative Activities for Chapter 20

COMPARING

Have students create a table foldable and label the rows and columns as shown. Students should list facts about the geography and economics of the three regions of Mexico in the appropriate spaces on the table. By completing this foldable, students will compare the geography and economic activities of northern Mexico, central Mexico, and southern Mexico.

MEXICO	Geography	Economics
Northern Mexico		
Central Mexico		
Southern Mexico		

HISTORY	Culture	Accomplishments
Olmec		
Maya		
Aztec		

ORGANIZING

Mexico's Native American heritage has shaped the country's culture. Encourage students to differentiate three important Native American civilizations of Mexico by creating this table foldable and labeling it as shown. Students should describe the culture and accomplishments of each of these civilizations in the appropriate spaces on the table.

Student Study Tip

Creating test questions (with correct answers) is a good way to review chapter material and prepare for tests. Encourage students to quiz each other about the facts of Chapter 20. Each student should create a 10-question quiz, then exchange quizzes with another classmate. Students should then grade each other's quizzes using the answer keys that they have already created.

Chapter 20 FOLDABLES

Central America and the West Indies

CHAPTER SUMMARY

Central America is made up of these seven countries: Belize, Honduras, Guatemala, El Salvador, Costa Rica, Nicaragua, and Panama. Although the mountainous areas are cool year-round, Central America is mostly tropical. Most people in the region either work on plantations or are subsistence farmers. Central America is a blend of both Native American and Spanish language and culture. In 1492 Christopher Columbus landed in the West Indies; the Spaniards permanently settled in 1496. The region is a mix of Native American, African, Asian, and European influences. The islands of the West Indies rely on tourism to support their economies. The West Indian government is democratic with the exception of Cuba, the only Communist nation in the Western Hemisphere.

CHAPTER PREVIEW

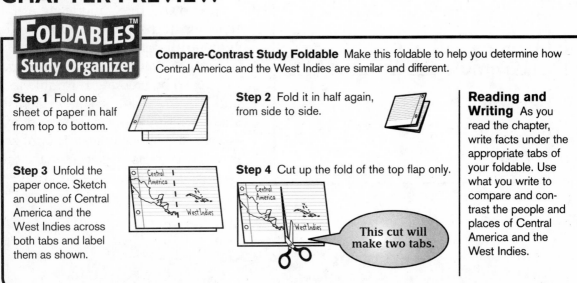

FOLDABLES™
Study Organizer

Compare-Contrast Study Foldable Make this foldable to help you determine how Central America and the West Indies are similar and different.

Step 1 Fold one sheet of paper in half from top to bottom.

Step 2 Fold it in half again, from side to side.

Reading and Writing As you read the chapter, write facts under the appropriate tabs of your foldable. Use what you write to compare and contrast the people and places of Central America and the West Indies.

Step 3 Unfold the paper once. Sketch an outline of Central America and the West Indies across both tabs and label them as shown.

Step 4 Cut up the fold of the top flap only.

This cut will make two tabs.

CHAPTER REVIEW

Foldables Follow-Up Activity

Have students create an outline map of Central America and the West Indies on poster board or on the blackboard. The map should be big enough for the entire class to work on it together. Have volunteers label each country. Then have students in turn write a fact about a country on the map using the information they have written in their completed foldables.

Alternative Activities for Chapter 21

EVALUATING

Have students create and label a foldable as shown. Students will compare and contrast the farming economies and the tourist-based economies found in Central America and the West Indies. As students read the chapter, they should write facts under each appropriate tab of their foldable. After completing their foldables, ask students to list the pros and cons of each type of economy.

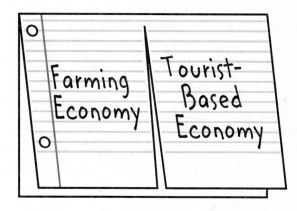

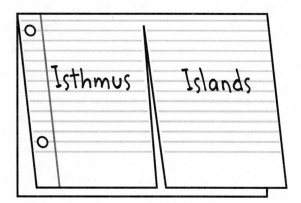

DESCRIBING

Have students create and label the foldable as shown. Students will use this foldable to describe how the isthmus of Central America differs from the islands of the West Indies. Students' descriptions should include a definition of *isthmus* and *island*, an example of each, and the characteristics that make these physical features similar and different.

Student Study Tip

Chapter 21 contains many facts. To help students remember what they have read, discuss some memorization techniques that they could use while studying. *Association*, or relating ideas to one another, will help them remember information. When students *visualize* as they read about different countries and their characteristics, they form mental images, which allows for better retention.

Chapter 21 FOLDABLES

Brazil and Its Neighbors

CHAPTER SUMMARY

Brazil is a large country with many resources, a lively culture, and serious economic challenges. Brazil declared its independence in 1822 after centuries of colonial rule by Portugal. Brazil is trying to reduce its number of poor people and balance the use of resources with the preservation of its rain forests. Brazil's neighbors—Argentina, Uruguay, Paraguay, Venezuela, Guyana, Suriname and French Guiana—have a diverse array of landforms, climates, and cultures.

CHAPTER PREVIEW

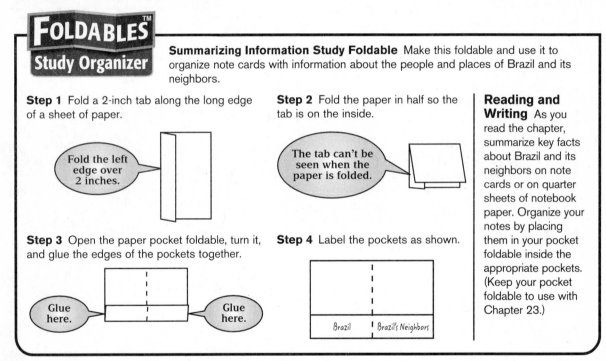

FOLDABLES™
Study Organizer

Summarizing Information Study Foldable Make this foldable and use it to organize note cards with information about the people and places of Brazil and its neighbors.

Step 1 Fold a 2-inch tab along the long edge of a sheet of paper.

Fold the left edge over 2 inches.

Step 2 Fold the paper in half so the tab is on the inside.

The tab can't be seen when the paper is folded.

Step 3 Open the paper pocket foldable, turn it, and glue the edges of the pockets together.

Glue here.   Glue here.

Step 4 Label the pockets as shown.

Brazil | Brazil's Neighbors

Reading and Writing As you read the chapter, summarize key facts about Brazil and its neighbors on note cards or on quarter sheets of notebook paper. Organize your notes by placing them in your pocket foldable inside the appropriate pockets. (Keep your pocket foldable to use with Chapter 23.)

CHAPTER REVIEW

Foldables Follow-Up Activity

Have students form groups of three to four. After students have assembled in their groups, have them share the information they collected in their pocket foldables with one another. Students should take turns reading aloud the facts they have collected. After each student reads a fact, the other students in the group should try to guess which country is being described. As a class, discuss the similarities and differences among the different countries.

Alternative Activities for Chapter 22

PROBLEM SOLVING

Have students create this pocket foldable and label it as shown. Students should collect information on note cards or on quarter sheets of paper about the history and current situation of the rain forest in Brazil. Advise students to include information about tourism, economic development, and the peoples of the rain forest. You may want to have students use the information they have collected to write a "letter to the editor" about how to preserve the rain forest.

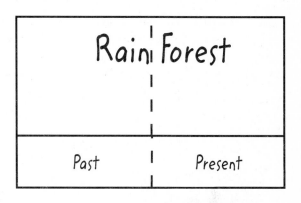

Rain Forest

Past | Present

South America:
Exploration and Colonization

Spain in South America | Portugal in South America

CAUSE AND EFFECT

Have students create a pocket foldable and label it as shown. Students should research the exploration and colonization of South America by Spain and Portugal. Have students take notes on index cards and collect them in their pocket foldables. As a class, discuss how South America's history has influenced its economic development.

Student Study Tip

As students study the chapter, remind them that they can use the images in the textbook to help them understand the material. Have students examine the photographs and graphics in the chapter and explain why they are included. Ask: What concept does each image illustrate? Students should summarize the information presented in the graphics as they take notes.

Chapter 22 **FOLDABLES**

The Andean Countries

CHAPTER SUMMARY

Colombia faces political and economic turmoil as a result of a civil war that has lasted for more than 35 years. Most Colombians are Roman Catholic and speak Spanish. Colombia's neighbors, Peru and Ecuador, share similar landscapes, climates, and history. The Inca developed a powerful and sophisticated civilization in the area that is now Peru. Bolivia and Chile share the Andes, but their economies and people are different. Chile has a diverse economy that includes mining, farming, and manufacturing. Bolivia is a poor country consisting mainly of the Andes and a high plateau, which is difficult to farm.

CHAPTER PREVIEW

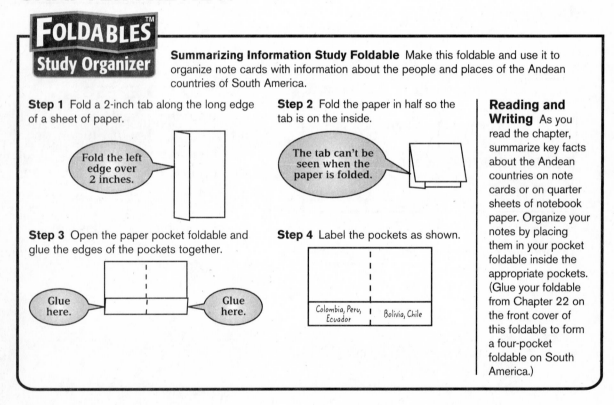

FOLDABLES™
Study Organizer

Summarizing Information Study Foldable Make this foldable and use it to organize note cards with information about the people and places of the Andean countries of South America.

Step 1 Fold a 2-inch tab along the long edge of a sheet of paper.

Fold the left edge over 2 inches.

Step 2 Fold the paper in half so the tab is on the inside.

The tab can't be seen when the paper is folded.

Step 3 Open the paper pocket foldable and glue the edges of the pockets together.

Glue here.   Glue here.

Step 4 Label the pockets as shown.

Colombia, Peru, Ecuador | Bolivia, Chile

Reading and Writing As you read the chapter, summarize key facts about the Andean countries on note cards or on quarter sheets of notebook paper. Organize your notes by placing them in your pocket foldable inside the appropriate pockets. (Glue your foldable from Chapter 22 on the front cover of this foldable to form a four-pocket foldable on South America.)

CHAPTER REVIEW

Foldables Follow-Up Activity

Have students work in pairs, sharing facts about the Andean countries that they have collected in their pocket foldables. Encourage them to pay attention to the similarities and differences in the facts they wrote. Students should take turns reciting the facts they wrote and explain why they thought these facts were important.

Alternative Activities for Chapter 23

IDENTIFYING OPTIONS

Have students create a pocket foldable like the one shown. Then have students write facts on note cards or on quarter sheets of paper, using their foldables to store them. Students should write facts about the political and economic challenges facing Colombia. After students have completed their foldables, discuss as a class the reasons for the challenges and have students provide possible solutions.

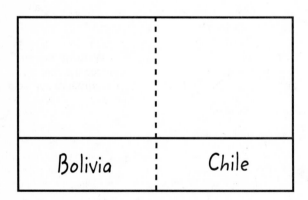

COMPARE AND CONTRAST

Have students create this foldable to compare and contrast two countries profiled in Chapter 23. Students should write facts about the countries on the note cards or on quarter sheets of paper and collect them in their pocket foldables. Have students use the information in their foldables to create a Venn diagram that compares and contrasts the two countries.

Student Study Tip

After reading and taking notes on a section of the textbook, remind students to stop and take a short break. They should then go back and reread the notes. Students should ask themselves: Is there anything that is unclear? Do any facts seem incorrect? Students should go back and clarify their notes as needed.

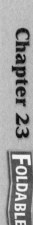

Chapter 23 **FOLDABLES**

Australia and New Zealand

CHAPTER SUMMARY

Australia is both a continent and a country. It has many natural resources but few people. The continent's land is mostly flat and dry, with little rainfall. Most of Australia's wealth comes from minerals and the products of its ranches. It is the world's leading producer and exporter of wool. New Zealand is a small country with a growing economy based on trade. Wool and lamb meat are New Zealand's major exports, and sheepherding is an important economic activity. Most New Zealanders live on North Island, where the country's two main cities, Auckland and Wellington, are located.

CHAPTER PREVIEW

Making Predictions Study Foldable Make this foldable to record information about Australia and New Zealand, which you will use to make predictions about the future of the countries.

Step 1 Fold one sheet of paper in half from top to bottom.

Step 2 Fold it in half again, from side to side.

Reading and Writing As you read the chapter, write what you learn about these countries under the appropriate tabs of your foldable. Then use that information to make predictions about the future economic growth and development of these countries.

Step 3 Unfold the paper once. Sketch an outline of Australia and New Zealand across the front tabs and label your foldable as shown.

Step 4 Cut up the fold of the top flap only.

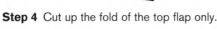

This cut will make two tabs.

CHAPTER REVIEW

Foldables Follow-Up Activity

Have students work in small groups to share their predictions about the future economic growth and development of Australia and New Zealand. Have students discuss the reasons for their predictions. Then have groups present their predictions to the class. You may want to hold a class vote to see whether class members agree or disagree with each prediction. Assign students the task of finding a newspaper article about one of the countries to see where it stands today.

Alternative Activities for Chapter 24

IDENTIFYING

Australia is both a continent and a country. As students read Section 1, have them write information under each appropriate tab of the foldable. Under each tab, students should explain why Australia is identified as a continent and a country. After they have completed their foldables, have students discuss the facts they found with a partner.

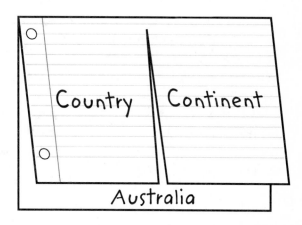

ANALYZING

Have students investigate Australia's Aborigine people and New Zealand's Maori people by creating and completing this foldable. Encourage them to include information about the history, culture, and economics of the Aborigines and Maori under each appropriate tab of their foldable. As a class, discuss the information the students found. Ask students if they think the Aborigines and the Maori have a history similar to any groups of people in the United States.

Student Study Tip

Advise students to read the chapter through, then go back and create an outline for it. Review the format of outlines with students. Main ideas are labeled with Roman numerals. Subtopics under each main idea are labeled with capital letters, and supporting details under each subtopic are labeled with Arabic numerals. Students should use the different headings in their textbooks to create their outlines.

Chapter 24

FOLDABLES

Oceania and Antarctica

CHAPTER SUMMARY

Oceania is made up of thousands of Pacific Ocean islands organized into countries and territories. Oceania can be divided into three main island regions—Melanesia, Micronesia, and Polynesia. Papua New Guinea, in Melanesia, is the largest and most populated country of Oceania. Most people of Oceania are descendants of people who left Southeast Asia on canoes thousands of years ago. The main economic activities are farming and tourism. Antarctica is a harsh land of rock and ice, which the world's nations have agreed to leave open to scientific study. Antarctica lies at the southern end of the earth. It is a major center of scientific research, but is the only continent with no permanent human population.

CHAPTER PREVIEW

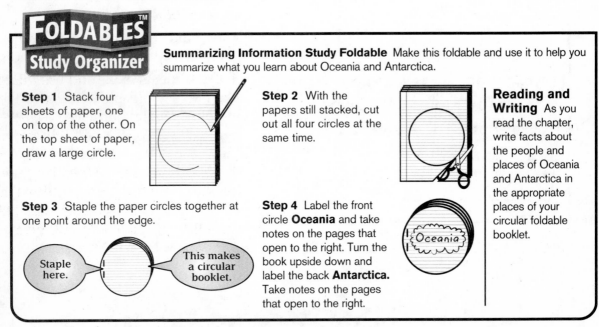

FOLDABLES™
Study Organizer

Summarizing Information Study Foldable Make this foldable and use it to help you summarize what you learn about Oceania and Antarctica.

Step 1 Stack four sheets of paper, one on top of the other. On the top sheet of paper, draw a large circle.

Step 2 With the papers still stacked, cut out all four circles at the same time.

Reading and Writing As you read the chapter, write facts about the people and places of Oceania and Antarctica in the appropriate places of your circular foldable booklet.

Step 3 Staple the paper circles together at one point around the edge.

Staple here.

This makes a circular booklet.

Step 4 Label the front circle **Oceania** and take notes on the pages that open to the right. Turn the book upside down and label the back **Antarctica.** Take notes on the pages that open to the right.

Oceania

CHAPTER REVIEW

Foldables Follow-Up Activity

Organize students into two groups and form lines facing each other. Designate one group as "Oceania" and the other group as "Antarctica." Starting at the beginning of one line, have each student recite one fact about the assigned region from his or her foldable. A student from the opposite line should respond by citing one fact from his or her assigned region. Continue this process until students are unable to cite any more facts. The team who cites the most facts wins.

Alternative Activities for Chapter 25

CATEGORIZING

Have students make and use this circular foldable booklet to describe the three regions of Oceania: Melanesia, Micronesia, and Polynesia. Students should label the front of the booklet *Oceania*, and then place the three regions as the headings on the next three pages of the booklet. On each page, students should list facts about the history, people, and culture of the region. As a class, discuss the information students wrote in their foldables.

Three Regions of Oceania

The Science of Antarctica

ORGANIZING

Have students make and use this circular booklet foldable to research the science of Antarctica and write about its land, plants, animals, and climate. Have students reread or review Section 2, taking notes about the information they find. Advise students to organize their notes on the pages of the booklet. Have students summarize why Antarctica is important to the study of science.

Student Study Tip

As students are reading the chapter, have them create profiles about each island and region. For example, students may want to draw the country's flag and note information about its population, economy, and government. Have students share their profiles with the rest of the class. Let students know that creating country profiles can be another good form of note taking.

Chapter 25 FOLDABLES